reach

reach

Create the Biggest
Possible Audience
for Your Message,
Book, or Cause

BECKY ROBINSON

BK

Berrett–Koehler Publishers, Inc.

Berrett-Koehler Publishers, Inc.
1333 Broadway, Suite 1000
Oakland, CA 94612-1921
Tel: (510) 817-2277
Fax: (510) 817-2278
www.bkconnection.com

ORDERING INFORMATION

Quantity sales. Special discounts are available on quantity purchases by corporations, associations, and others. For details, contact the "Special Sales Department" at the Berrett-Koehler address above.

Individual sales. Berrett-Koehler publications are available through most bookstores. They can also be ordered directly from Berrett-Koehler: Tel: (800) 929-2929; Fax: (802) 864-7626; www.bkconnection.com.

Orders for college textbook / course adoption use. Please contact Berrett-Koehler: Tel: (800) 929-2929; Fax: (802) 864-7626.

Distributed to the U.S. trade and internationally by Penguin Random House Publisher Services.

Berrett-Koehler and the BK logo are registered trademarks of Berrett-Koehler Publishers, Inc.

Printed in Canada

Berrett-Koehler books are printed on long-lasting acid-free paper. When it is available, we choose paper that has been manufactured by environmentally responsible processes. These may include using trees grown in sustainable forests, incorporating recycled paper, minimizing chlorine in bleaching, or recycling the energy produced at the paper mill.

Library of Congress Cataloging-in-Publication Data

Names: Robinson, Becky, author.
Title: Reach : create the biggest possible audience for your message, book, or cause / Becky Robinson.
Description: First Edition. | Oakland, CA : Berrett-Koehler Publishers, [2022] | Includes bibliographical references and index.
Identifiers: LCCN 2021050951 (print) | LCCN 2021050952 (ebook) | ISBN 9781523000876 (paperback) | ISBN 9781523000883 (pdf) | ISBN 9781523000890 (epub)
Subjects: LCSH: Social media—Marketing. | Internet marketing. | Consumer behavior.
Classification: LCC HF5414 .R53 2022 (print) | LCC HF5414 (ebook) | DDC 658.8/72—dc23/eng/20211210
LC record available at https://lccn.loc.gov/2021050951
LC ebook record available at https://lccn.loc.gov/2021050952

First Edition
28 27 26 25 24 23 22   10 9 8 7 6 5 4 3 2 1

Book design and production: Seventeenth Street Studios
Cover design and illustration: Rachel Royer

To my family

Contents

foreword

Try not to become a person of success, but rather try to become a person of value.

ALBERT EINSTEIN

When Becky Robinson and I met in 2011, I was working in Boston at the Disruptive Innovation Fund, which I co-founded with Clayton and Matt Christensen. I was about to launch my first book, *Dare, Dream, Do: Remarkable Things Happen When You Dare to Dream.* I had dared to write a book but I didn't know what to do next.

Through a timely stroke of good fortune, Jesse Lyn Stoner, a mutual friend, connected us. Becky lived in Michigan and was in the process of reentering the workforce. First-time author, me, became Becky's first client at Weaving Influence. It was a wonderful partnership for which I will always be grateful.

As Becky taught me how to extend my reach, I watched as she expanded hers.

Becky had joined Facebook and learned social media marketing after several years of being out of the paid workforce. That led to an opportunity as a social media marketing director for a leadership consultant who had just published a book. This led to the founding of her online marketing firm, Weaving Influence. Today, a decade later, her company has twelve employees and as many contractors and is a thriving business that has launched hundreds of books, including some by renowned authors such as Ken Blanchard, Mark Miller, and Cheryl Bachelder.

One of the magical things about Becky Robinson is that she walks her talk. She consistently provides value related to online influence and has for ten years. She is incredibly generous and always willing to share her expertise. She demonstrates the Four Commitments she writes about in her book (value, consistency, generosity, and longevity). And whether you meet her in person, online, or on the pages of this book, you will feel like you are having a conversation with a personal coach and cheerleader all in one.

What I love most about *Reach* is that Becky isn't hawking fame. Some of you may become famous, but that's not the promise of the book nor is it ultimately the goal. Fame does not guarantee that an individual's work will be of value to others. Becky's goal is for anyone with a message to be heard by the people who want and need to hear it. She wants everyone's voice to have the opportunity to do the job it is meant to do. That's her promise and she keeps it.

If you care deeply about sharing your life's work and message, if you want to make a greater contribution to the world, if you want to reach the people who need to hear what only you can say, start reading, start highlighting, and start following Becky Robinson's advice now.

Whitney Johnson
Lexington, Virginia
September 6, 2021

How Far Can You Reach?

I landed on the title *Reach* for this book while out running one day. We'd been going back and forth about titles and I'd headed out to run and wait for inspiration. With every footfall, I thought about you, one of the people who would read my book, and what you would most want. When the word "reach" popped into my mind, I stopped my watch, grabbed my phone, and texted my husband. We had found our title.

I'm not sure how you measure and define reach or what it means to you, but I know you want more of it. For the purpose of this book, I'm defining reach in a new way. Reach is not only about creating the biggest possible audience for your work, as the subtitle promises. It's also about the lasting impact your work can have. Reach means expanding your audience plus having a lasting impact.

This book does not offer a fast path to fame or fortune. If you're looking for that, this book may not be for you. However, if you're willing to invest resources in sharing your valuable work online, consistently over time for a long time, and give of yourself generously to others, you'll find that your audience and your impact will expand.

reach
=
Expanding Audience
+
Lasting Impact

FIGURE 1. The Reach Equation

Reach and Fame

If you're not already famous, it's important to have a realistic view of what is possible, especially if you are just starting out. This is true whether you have a book to promote, an idea you want to draw attention to, or a cause you're passionate about. If you are just beginning, prepare yourself to work over the long term to create lasting impact. There is no express train to reach.

Consider how reach relates to books. There's a reason traditional publishers look carefully at an author's platform to see how many people follow them before they offer a book deal. The survival of publishing companies is tied to making the right bets on which books to publish and which books to pass up.

Most of the books that make it to the *New York Times* best-seller lists each year come from authors whose names were already widely known before their publisher agreed to publish their new book. Publishers want to offer books from well-known authors with a track record of selling thousands of books year after year or books by celebrities or politicians. Barack Obama's first book release after leaving the presidency sold 887,000 copies on the first day.[1]

Publishers want to publish a sure thing. If you're not a sure thing, you'll need to make a strong case for your ability to sell books to an existing group of fans or followers. Don't worry, you don't have to be able to prove you can sell a million copies. Many independent or smaller publishers only want you to prove you can make enough money at first to break even on the project. From there, they want to know that your book can be profitable over its lifetime. An initial print run for a nonfiction business title might be 3,000 to 5,000 copies. If you can sell those within the first six to nine months after publication, you earn a reprint. If you sell out the reprint, you'll be among the more successful titles the publisher releases that year. For the authors we serve in the business book space, selling more than 10,000 copies in a year represents significant success.

The Famous Few

What I find is that almost anyone who has a passion for their work wants to create as much reach as possible. We all want our products to be the next big thing, our causes to be widely recognized and supported, and our ideas to reach the entire globe. Authors look to emulate the success of a small number of hardworking people who have become best sellers.

Fueled by energy and ambition, creators overlook or underplay the huge investment needed to achieve the breakout success they strive toward. They may expect to achieve success at the outset that others accumulate over decades.

The fact is that people typically write more than a few books before they reach the level where they sell millions. John Maxwell, who has written nearly 100 books at the time of this writing, has sold more than 20 million copies of his books. Ken Blanchard, another of the most prolific business book authors in the world, has sold over 13 million copies of the more than 60 books he has in print. Brené Brown, who has authored more than 7 books, has sold nearly 5 million copies.

The most well-known business book authors on the planet—Patrick Lencioni, Stephen Covey, Seth Godin, Simon Sinek, Daniel H. Pink, Adam Grant—have all published multiple books over many years. Even Grant, the youngest on my list at age 40, has four major titles on his résumé.

You might note that every single one of these best-known business book authors is white and male. Marginalized groups face unique challenges in creating reach for their messages. It is imperative that people from dominant identities work to include, support, and celebrate emerging voices.

Every author I meet wants to achieve the success of these famous few and every client I serve who is not an author wants to achieve widespread awareness of their work and ideas. In most instances, they do not want fame and fortune; instead, they seek meaning, purpose, and a desire to make a difference through their life and work. People who bring great passion to their work also bring a deep desire to share their work with others.

Brené Brown (brenebrown.com) is the person the authors, thought leaders, nonprofit leaders, and coaches I've served over the past decade most want to emulate. Brown is well known for having sold many millions of books during her career as an author. She has been on the *New York Times* best-seller list five times, and her TED Talk from 2012 went viral.[2] Her enviable speaking career has expanded with each book release. Did you know that Brown published her first book in 2004, several years after beginning her work in the field? Her contribution through speaking, researching, teaching, and publishing spans more than two decades.

While Brown is widely known, loved, and followed, hers is not a universally recognized household name despite her tremendous success and contribution.

When first-time authors hope to reach Brown's level of success with their first book release, they are discounting the massive value she has poured into her work consistently over decades to produce the results she now enjoys.

Very few of us can catapult to those results without making a similar long-term investment.

It's not unusual for me to meet an author who tells me that their goal is to sell a half a million books in the first two years. Although I don't want to be a dream crusher, a goal of this magnitude is not realistic for most people seeking to build a platform. My company has launched more than 150 books, and even though I've partnered with very smart and interesting people who have huge ambition, I have yet to see a book reach that half-million mark in sales. While it's always possible that you could be the one who will write and publish that breakout book—the one that achieves massive sales without decades of preparation on your part—it's not likely.

The big goals many people set get in the way of their working toward more reasonable success in spreading their ideas and selling their books. Creators get so focused on making it big that they neglect the simple, quiet ways to make a difference. They miss the chance to follow through on the everyday activities that will expand the reach of their ideas.

One of the most successful titles I've supported since I began partnering with authors, *Help Them Grow or Watch Them Go: Career Conversations Employees Want* (2012) by Beverly Kaye (bevkaye.com) and Julie Winkle Giulioni (juliewinklegiulioni.com), has been published in two editions, has been translated into six languages, and has sold 120,000 copies—but that happened over eight years. Kaye has sold over a million books in her lifetime, including over 800,000 copies of her classic book *Love 'Em or Lose 'Em: Getting Good People to Stay* (1999), yet her name is unknown to most outside the career development and organizational development spaces she's worked in. While Kaye may not be among the famous few and has not landed on any well-known best-seller lists, her work has achieved massive reach by any definition.

When Winkle Giulioni joined Kaye as a first-time author, she did not have an online presence at all. Yet over the years since her book's release, she has chosen to share content online through her own blog and other online publications. Winkle Giulioni has seen that the value she's added through her online presence has created countless opportunities for her to get paid well to do the work she loves: speaking, consulting, and writing.[3] Julie is also achieving reach.

How to Create the Greatest Possible Reach for Your Work

What if instead of aspiring to be one of the famous few like Brené Brown, you aspired to influence as many people as you can through your work? Most of the millions of books written and published each year are written by people whose names you don't know. Most nonprofits are led by people whose names you'll never hear. If most people won't ever be famous, why not instead make up your mind to make the largest impact possible through your ideas, books, or cause?

> Reach is never static; it is the product of what you do to expand your work and its impact over time.

We tend to think of followers or fans or an audience as a relatively stable commodity attached to a public figure. Reach does not work this way. It is more intangible and dynamic, the interplay of your growing audience and their long-term investment in you. You may have the same size email list as someone else in your field, but you will have greater reach if your emails are opened more quickly, with more excitement, and with more follow-up actions over time. Reach is never static; it is the product of what you do to expand your work and its impact over time.

This kind of reach is achievable only when you make four commitments, which I'll weave throughout this book.

In order to create reach, you'll need to commit to value, consistency, longevity, and generosity. The people whose stories I share in the book demonstrate the results you can achieve when you incorporate the commitments. Throughout the book, we'll use the icons below to draw your attention to the concepts of value, consistency, longevity, and generosity.

Defining reach only quantitatively, which people often do, overlooks the ultimate goal of making a difference through their work. Think, for example, about a video that goes viral. The creator has grabbed the attention of millions of people for as long as their momentary fame lasts. But if the impression they have made is not translated into

◈ VALUE

↻ CONSISTENCY

∞ LONGEVITY

♥ GENEROSITY

FIGURE 2. The Reach Commitments Key

an ongoing connection, their success is fleeting. The reach I describe in this book grows, expands, and lasts.

Value

◈ Reach starts with delivering value to people. Clarity is an important component of value. You want to create a message people will remember and you want to be a messenger people will remember. Throughout the book, value is represented by a diamond icon.

Value is determined by the recipient of the content. It is the right message for the right need at the right time. For a parent who is navigating the changes involved as their children graduate from high school and move on to making adult decisions, Grown and Flown Parents, a Facebook group numbering more than 200,000, creates significant value.[4]

Creating value begins with a decision to share your thoughts, ideas, perspectives, approaches, and insights with others. You promote these ideas online in various formats so people will engage with you by reading, listening, or watching what you have to share because they find value in what you're creating. Your work in the world will become meaningful to those who choose to learn from and interact with you.

Consistency

⟳ Throughout the book, I'll tell you about people who have successfully created expansive reach for their work. Without fail, you'll see that consistency in creating and sharing value with others is important to their success.

Tiffany Roe (tiffanyroe.com), a counselor and podcaster from Utah who calls herself the original Instagram therapist, demonstrates the value of consistency through her online presence. Since she began her counseling practice in 2015, she has grown a following of over 125,000 people on Instagram. Roe posts positive mental health advice multiple times each day as she seeks to "change the mental health game" and help people "feel, deal, heal."[5]

While consistency sounds like a great idea, good intentions to create a consistent online presence can easily get derailed. The key to creating consistency is creating a sustainable approach. Throughout the book, consistency is represented by a circle made by arrows.

Longevity

∞ The stories I'll share throughout the book illustrate the importance of longevity in creating reach. It takes time to build connections and create momentum for your message, book, or cause. People who seek a quick formula for achieving reach often do not understand the importance and value of sticking around. Many people give up too quickly instead of patiently building to create results.

A long-term view is needed if you want to create lasting impact. Think about the respect and deference we give to longtime employees of a company or to a baseball player who stays with a franchise long enough to become a legend. Throughout the book, longevity is represented by an infinity symbol.

Tim Sackett (timsackett.com), a human resources and talent acquisitions expert, has blogged daily for over a decade. His longevity on his website has helped grow his reach and influence.[6]

Ann Voskamp (annvoskamp.com), the author of four *New York Times* best sellers, began blogging in 2004.[7] In 2006, when I sent off an email to her as a fan of her blog, she was still years away from the release of her debut memoir in 2011. While the value of Ann's work certainly expanded her reach, her longevity has ensured that she continues to have an impact nearly two decades after she began publishing reflections online from her farm in Canada.

Generosity

♥ The journey to creating reach and impact for your work is fueled by generosity, both given and received. Making meaning and making a difference is impossible without a desire to give to others. In this book, you'll hear about different ways of expressing generosity and about how giving more away is a helpful way to reach more people.

Steve Burda, whom *Business Insider* has called the most connected person on LinkedIn, says his commitment and dedication to others' success is responsible for his success. Focusing on others instead of yourself is generosity.[8]

When I sent Ann Voskamp an email in 2006 inquiring about a geography curriculum she'd written for homeschooling parents, she responded by sending me a free copy of the curriculum without any expectation of return. She created a lifelong fan.

Generosity is powerful because it is unexpected, disarming, and unforgettable. Throughout the book, generosity is represented by a heart icon.

Making a Difference without Being Famous

Here's a story from my life about the reach that can be created through an online presence. In the spring of 2016, I hosted a booth at the Association for Talent Development International Conference in Denver, Colorado. Having

previously attended several ATD conferences, I knew
there'd be lots of business luminaries there. In past
years, I'd met Jim Kouzes, Marshall Goldsmith, and Ken
Blanchard, all people I admired and considered famous. I
knew I wasn't at all famous.

Imagine my delight when someone stopped me to talk
as I walked through the busy exposition. "Becky Robinson,"
someone said. "I've attended your webinars." A few hours
later, the same thing happened again. People I didn't know
personally but who had received value from my work in
the world cared enough to acknowledge and appreciate
me. At an event where plenty of more influential, famous,
exciting, or well-known people were present, people cared
about talking to me. My work had reached them.

I'm not famous in the world's eyes, but I can make a difference as I share value generously and consistently over
time. As I share value day after day, year after year, I am
contributing in a way that makes the world a better place
for everyone and I am seeing my work have its largest possible impact.

Five Hundred Trees

In 2016, my family and I moved from a subdivision to a
home on a five-acre plot not too far from town. We bought
the home from the Sitarskis, who bought this land in the
early 1990s when a farm field filled the space between the
house and the road. The Sitarskis had a vision of creating a peaceful retreat, a private escape. If they had had an
unlimited budget, they could have invested in mature trees
to quickly create the privacy they desired, but as the parents of three growing kids, their landscaping budget was
too small to do that.

Instead, the Sitarskis bought 500 saplings. The kids joined in and painstakingly planted each of the trees around the property. They watered, fertilized, and pruned them. Nearly thirty years later when we drove down the quarter-mile driveway to tour what would become our new home, tall pines stood guard on the edge of the property, oaks and maples lined the driveway, and woods surrounded the large open backyard. Those 500 trees (and likely more over the years) had grown to become the peaceful retreat the Sitarskis had envisioned.

Whatever your goal is, if it involves making a positive difference in the world and contributing to others through your ideas, your message, your book, or your cause, consider the long-term view. If you choose to invest in contributing value to the world over time, you are like the family who planted 500 trees and waited for them to grow. You will certainly enjoy the benefits of contributing along the way. You may also be building value that people will enjoy and appreciate even long after you are gone.

If you choose to be one who plants 500 trees and waits for them to grow, you will become famous to a few who choose to listen to you, read your work, or participate in your cause.

Who This Book Is For

Reach is a book for anyone who wants to create greater impact for their ideas, message, book, or cause. It's okay if you want to have a huge impact. You will if you are willing to commit to a consistent approach over time. ↻

You may be discouraged about your current traction or feel the temptation to compare your current reach to others who seem more influential. We all start somewhere. When you're getting started, you may be famous to only a few. As you show up consistently in online spaces, sharing value with those who most need your message, you be able to influence more and more people over time. When you start, you may know everyone who is paying attention to you online. In the early days of writing my first blog, I could name each person who regularly commented on my posts; they were the few who read my work and knew my name. Yet over time, you will begin to be known by many more people who know, remember, recommend, and celebrate your work—your influence will grow and your reach will expand.

While you may never be famous worldwide, the only way to have the biggest impact for your messages is to do the hard work over time. ∞

This book is for you

- if you are just beginning to share content in online spaces and want to secure greater reach for your work.

- if you have been looking to grow traction for your idea, book, or cause but are frustrated about your results and are not sure how to create additional success.

- if you're making progress with online influence but you want to create a more sustainable and consistent approach to online marketing.

- if you have contributed to the world significantly but haven't invested in sharing content online.

A special note if you have built significant value in the world through your work but haven't invested in building your online presence: You have a choice about whether to invest your time online. You may feel that it's too late or that learning online marketing is too overwhelming and difficult. It's likely that your online footprint consists of what others have written about you instead of what you yourself have written. Investing in building your own presence online is a chance to tell your own story and highlight what matters most to you so that people can benefit over the long term from your life's work. When you choose to bring the real-world reputation and credibility you've built offline into online spaces, you can secure a lasting legacy for your most important ideas.

How to Read This Book

You can read the book from start to finish or you can skip to the chapters that interest you. As you read, look out for the Four Commitment icons. The questions and resources at the end of each chapter will inform additional study and reflection. I've also included an appendix and a group discussion guide at the end of the book. To download all the extra learning resources and find links to all the resources mentioned throughout the book, visit beckyrobinson.com/reachbook or scan the QR code at the end of each chapter.

Getting Started

Most of us are not famous and will never be. However, you can make a significant difference in the world if you choose to show up in online spaces where you share valuable content and ideas. ◈ As you do so, you will create the greatest possible impact for your work. Over time, if you invest patiently and consistently, you will create wider reach for your work and ideas. ↻ You'll become more well known and you'll experience the benefits of a growing online presence. Those you are serving will benefit also. The more you give, the more you'll gain. ♥

FOR REFLECTION

- What do you most want to accomplish with your idea, message, book, or cause?
- How do you define success?
- What does reach mean to you?
- Who, if anyone, are you reaching now?
- What time, energy, and financial resources are you willing to share to increase the reach of your ideas?
- Would you be willing to plant 500 trees for future generations to enjoy?

Additional Resources

Listen to my podcast conversation with Julie Winkle Giulioni and download a graphic of the definition of reach from this chapter.

chapter 1

Evaluating Your Current Approach to Building Traction for Your Message

"Stefani Germanotta, you will never be famous." This was the title of a Facebook group Germanotta's classmates at New York University started. Lady Gaga's peers disdained her audacious dreams.[1] A few years later, in 2010, Lady Gaga gave an interview to reporter Neil McCormick, who described her rise to fame as rapid, inexorable, and global. She told him, "I have always been an artist. And I've always been famous, you just didn't know it yet."[2]

Lady Gaga's story is not a common one. Her achievement of catapulting from coffeehouse gigs to worldwide best-selling artist status—she has won Grammys, Golden Globes, and an Academy Award, among other accolades and recognition—is unduplicated. And Lady Gaga didn't have a wealthy family, famous parents, or other support to buoy her talent. Instead, hard work and unique talent, extreme focus, and flamboyant costumes all contributed to her rise to fame. As the artist told McCormick, "There's a real art to fame."

To rise from obscurity to renown requires the perfect alignment of many factors: talent, hard work, great timing, a message or product with wide appeal, and a little bit of fairy dust.

If you are prolific enough and well known enough, you don't need to work to have your online presence match your offline contribution. The world will do the work for you. People who live public lives show up online through the efforts of others.

If you are not among those famous few, you will need to curate and cultivate your own story online in order to create meaning, impact, and reach over time.

Those of us who don't aspire to rock-star status and are seeking a different kind of renown for our work need to realize that there is no easy path to gaining traction for our book, business, cause, or message. Hard work as a precursor to influence and significance is an unavoidable reality.

> **You will need to curate and cultivate your own story online in order to create meaning, impact, and reach over time.**

Closing the Influence Gap

In my work with clients over the years, I've identified a significant gap that even very successful people must overcome to create reach. It's the difference between how a person shows up online and how they show up offline.

Most people naturally invest more time, energy, and resources in their offline lives. However, an exclusive focus on offline life will almost always limit reach.

The only way to create the biggest reach possible for your work is to grow your contributions online and offline simultaneously. Whatever you do, do it out loud, sharing the story of your work publicly so people can learn and benefit from your work even if they don't know you offline. Those who are on a journey with the goal of creating more impact need to maximize both their offline contributions and their online presence over time to reach more people. They need to share the value of their work both online and offline.

Categories of Online Presence

During my twelve years of working with people to increase the reach of their messages, I've identified four levels of expertise related to creating an online presence. Figure 3 illustrates these four levels. Each circle includes a globe icon (representing offline influence) and a computer screen icon (representing online influence).

Someone who has neither online nor offline influence is a beginner. Note that in the beginner circle of figure 3, both the globe icon and the computer screen icon are marked with an X, which indicates that both online and offline influence are absent. Someone who has influence online but not offline is a master of branding. In this circle, the

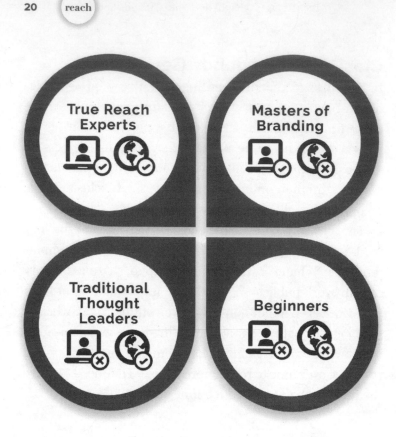

FIGURE 3. Levels of Influence

globe icon is marked with an X, indicating that people in this category do not have offline influence. Someone who has offline influence that is not fully represented online is a traditional thought leader. In this circle, the icon for online influence is marked with an X. The fourth circle depicts true reach experts, the people who show up online in the same powerful way that they show up in real life. People in this group are positioned to create the biggest possible audience and lasting impact for their work.

The Beginner

If you are at the start of your career or at the start of creating traction for an idea, message, book, or cause, you likely are in the category of beginner. You could also call yourself a beginning beginner. You have neither recognition offline nor impact online . . . yet. You're figuring out your brand position in life or figuring out your career journey. Or you've been in a career and you're making a switch but have little experience related to your aspirations.

There's no shame in being here. Instead of being overwhelmed about all that lies ahead, be inspired by the vision of what you can accomplish. There's nowhere to go but up from here. Throughout the book, I'll give you suggestions about how to start. Patience will be helpful on this journey, since starting to grow influence online is like planting a tree; it may be years before you enjoy the shade.

Everyone who is starting something new is in this group. In 2009, when I joined Facebook for the first time, I was in this category. I had stepped out of a job in a nonprofit organization when I had my first child in 2001. I didn't have a specific career vision and I didn't have any expertise to add to a topic or to a vision of where I could contribute. Even though I was approaching age 40, it would not have been a stretch to call me a beginning beginner.

It can be humbling to be in this place. After I started to take some freelance writing gigs, one of my clients approached me and asked me to write a leadership blog in support of the university's online leadership degree programs. He framed the request like this: "How would you feel about writing a blog about a topic you know nothing about?" The topic? Leadership.

I remember feeling annoyed. I told my client about my role as president of our condo association, the preschool co-op I had started, and the church I had partnered with my husband to start. "I know about leadership," I told him. But I really didn't. I had to start at the beginning. I had neither expertise to offer in the real world nor anything meaningful to say online. I had to work to create both at the same time.

As a beginner who wants to create lasting legacy for your work, it is critical that you first consider the four commitments of reach. You'll need to adopt a discovery-driven approach to creating value.

DISCOVER YOUR VALUE

◈ After I entered online spaces in 2009, I acquired more learning about leadership by teaching one semester of undergraduate courses in leadership for an online program. This short stint gave me some additional credibility, but only a thin veneer.

Along the way, I began experimenting with and learning about social media marketing. In my freelance work for the university, I started and grew a Twitter account, then started managing Facebook pages. At the time, we were all learning about social media together and I learned a lot by exploration and experimentation. Increasing my expertise about social media proved to be much easier than increasing my learning about leadership. I had so much catching up to do about being a leader.

When I started my own blog in 2010, my path as a digital marketing professional was still not yet clear. I envisioned writing about several topics: leadership, relational connections, and social media.

I had to experiment with topics in my online writing and posting until I had enough experience to see the path forward. I discovered along the way what topics excited me, what topics interested the people who read my work, and where I could make my most meaningful contribution, including how I could carve out a profitable and purposeful business.

Newcomers in online spaces can experiment with content first. They can learn from experience to clarify and hone in on how they can best contribute value.

ADD CONSISTENCY

↻ It will be impossible to create significance offline or online without consistency. Once you've identified how you will bring value, start contributing it consistently. So many people who start to build an online presence give up before they have a chance to break through to widespread success.

SETTLE IN

∞ As you are getting started, patience is imperative. Without patience, you will not sustain your contributions long enough to create reach.

Humility at the start may give you some early momentum. If you are just getting started, own it. Tell people "I'm new here. I'm just getting started."

When I started blogging about leadership in 2009, I spent a lot of time seeking out other leadership bloggers. Early on, I developed a friendship with several bloggers who'd been on the scene longer than me. I soon discovered that most of them had significantly more expertise than I did that added credibility to their contributions on leadership. I asked a lot of questions. I listened to and acted on their advice.

While I was establishing my brand, I had to ask for help—often. I remember an early win in May 2009. The blog I wrote at the time had been going for a few months.

I decided to reach out to Dan McCarthy, blogger at Great Leadership by Dan, to ask him to host a guest article. When he responded favorably, I danced and shrieked around my house. I had no idea how these humble beginnings would lead to my discovery of a powerful new career.

When you are just getting started and can ask for help and humbly learn from others, you can fuel ongoing collaborative relationships. People will want to be helpful and will appreciate the opportunity to guide your journey. Starting strong will increase your chances of sticking around long enough to make an impact.

BE GENEROUS

♥ One of the benefits of being a beginning beginner is that you are probably showing up in online spaces without an urgent agenda apart from learning and contributing. Because of this, you may have more time, energy, and willingness to promote others and their work. As a newcomer to online conversations on a certain topic, you can attract attention by amplifying the work and ideas of other people.

In this beginning stage and throughout your journey, be as generous as you can. Link to other people's work, quote other people, participate in promoting others' books or causes, write reviews of people's books. If you've learned from someone, acknowledge their contribution. If you admire someone, shout it out.

Masters of Branding

It's possible to build massive traction for your online presence without any substance behind your work, but any success that does not have value to support your brand will be short lived.

If you have achieved online reach before you've created depth in your content and vision, you can continue to fuel your online presence while you develop your ideas.

Often people who have online success without the offline significance to back up their online presence flare and then fizzle. Masters of branding may quickly grow a following or they may buy followers. They may look amazing on the level of surface metrics—the number of followers, fans, and likes they get. They may fill their feeds with beautiful photographs and messages that aren't clearly related to a core message.

To create impact, you have to bring substance, not superficiality. It's impossible to offer something meaningful if your work lacks meaning. I'm sure you can quickly think of people who are focused more on making money than on creating meaning. If you have a negative view of these people, it is likely because of their inauthenticity.

You probably bought this book because you have a real message to share and are motivated to offer value. You are in no danger of becoming a master of branding.

Traditional Thought Leaders

Many of the people I work with are traditional thought leaders. ◈ These are people who have created value through their books, their businesses, their ideas, or their messages but have not yet worked to build a significant online presence.

This is often because their contributions predate the internet. They began their contributions at a time when people gained traction for their ideas through the traditional modes of publishing, speaking, teaching, traveling, and gaining exposure in major media.

Traditional thought leaders may have great reach in organizations, institutions, and communities where they are well known for their contributions, but they may not have an online presence commensurate with their knowledge. They have not translated their offline reach into a similarly far-reaching online presence.

People who are traditional thought leaders are still contributing value to the world through their work. Below I highlight three generations of people who face the biggest challenges in replicating their offline success through their online presence. These three generations represent people who are now 44 and older; the generations who didn't grow up with digital tools. They may have been able to achieve great success and add tremendous value without creating thriving online communities.

While these generations may not need to invest in an online presence to achieve their goals, choosing not to show up online is a decision to limit their reach and influence. Investing in online presence can create greater reach for books, businesses, messages, or causes for people of any age.

LEGACY THOUGHT LEADERS

If you are age 75 or older, you may be in the legacy phase of your thought leadership and influence building. You may be publishing and contributing into your 80s and 90s.

If you Google the names of people in the legacy phase of their thought leadership, you may find a Wikipedia page or links to journal articles. You will find their books for sale on Amazon. You may find a website that they own, but it may not tell the whole story of their lives and contributions.

Bev Kaye's Story

Bev Kaye published her first book in 1982 with Prentice-Hall. Between that time and now, she's published five more books, most of which have been translated into other languages and reprinted in multiple editions, including the latest release of her 1999 book *Love 'Em or Lose 'Em: Getting Good People to Stay*, which is now in its sixth edition and has sold more than 800,000 copies worldwide.

For most of her career, Kaye relied on the strength of her in-person presence as a speaker, trainer, and consultant to expand the reach of her ideas and create opportunities for her business. For her, marketing each book meant showing up in the places where her readers gathered, including the annual conferences of the Association for Talent Development and the Society of Human Resource Management. "I marketed myself by being seen in a lot of places," she says. For Kaye, the priority of her in-person reputation has always superseded her online presence.

Kaye, who in 2021 is in her late 70s, continues to work with organizations as "a guide on the side and a sage on the stage." While she sees the importance of showing up online, she's still not comfortable using social media tools and relies on her staff to support her online presence.

"I am certainly turned on and tuned in to this work. And you know, by luck, I chose topics that have been evergreen for decades," Kaye shared. "They've morphed and they've changed. But the need for us to help people grow careers is still bigger than ever. And the need for people to be engaged and retained is as big as it ever was, if not more so. So I am getting blogs out and tweets out so this work can continue to spread in the world."[3]

BABY BOOMER THOUGHT LEADERS

People who were born in the period 1945 to 1964 may also have offline influence that outpaces their online presence. They may have been slow to adopt new technologies and adapt to reaching audiences online. They may be more comfortable picking up the phone than they are sending an email newsletter. They may have a strong preference for in-person, face-to-face meetings rather than virtual events.

These folks may still be in the midst of their full-time working years or could be moving toward retirement.

These thought leaders need to consider how enhancing their online presence will help them reach wider audiences for their messages while contributing to their overall success.

Ralph and Rich Brandt's Story

When I first met Ralph and Rich Brandt, twin brothers who co-founded RDR Group (rdrgroup.com), an organization that provides training on topics such as workplace harassment and diversity and inclusion, their goal was to grow their business to involve the next generation of their families. Rich hoped to involve his son, Adam, and Ralph hoped to continue a steady business so his daughters, Heidi and Cassi, whom he had already involved as trainers in RDR Group, could continue to provide valuable services to employers and organizations in the future.

RDR's past strategy for client acquisition involved calling possible client organizations. As that approach became increasingly ineffective, Ralph and Rich knew they needed to invest in building their brand online by converting their website from a virtual brochure to a dynamic resource where employers and directors of organizations could discover the value RDR offers.

RDR's shift to showing up online in more powerful ways came at a perfect time. When their in-person training business came to a screeching halt with the arrival of the Coronavirus, the team already had a vision for how to deliver their work virtually. One year after the advent of changes due to COVID, RDR Group had grown to the point where Adam Brandt could join RDR Group full time. The RDR Group story is evidence of the power of showing up online to increase the reach and success of a business.

MILES TO GO (GENERATION X)

Gen Xers grew up in the 1970s and 1980s. Some members of this generation entered the workforce before the widespread use of email, the internet, and other digital tools. Most are in the middle of their career and have miles to go on their career journeys and no plans to retire yet. Many are active on social media and are comfortable with technology even if they are not effectively leveraging these tools to expand their reach.

Many members of this generation may fall into the category of traditional thought leaders because they have focused on their offline careers at the expense of their online footprint. They may also have poured energy into growing the brand of their company or their employer instead of their personal brands. As a result, they have created great traction for the messages of their organizations online but have difficulty translating that reach once they leave the organization. I worked with a Gen Xer who exited her investor-backed start-up and realized that while her former company still had huge reach through its website and online presence, she was struggling to market her book because she had not built her own brand identity apart from that of her company.

Karin Hurt's Story

Karin Hurt (letsgrowleaders.com) is the coauthor with David Dye of *Winning Well* (2016) and *Courageous Cultures* (2020) and the CEO of Let's Grow Leaders. Hurt is a Gen Xer who spent the 1990s, the early part of her career, growing a solid reputation offline as a business leader and executive at Verizon Wireless. When I met Hurt in 2012, she had just begun blogging about leadership and bringing her extensive knowledge and experience to online spaces. ◈ Prior to building her brand online, Hurt fit into the category of a traditional thought leader. Now she is a true expert both online and offline. Here's a glimpse into how she made the transition.

Hurt started blogging while she was still an active executive who oversaw 10,000 people in seven different companies that Verizon Wireless outsourced to. While working with call center staff, Karin noticed herself telling the same stories. She decided to put advice into blog posts and invite her colleagues to read the blog. "What I did not really anticipate is that it would start to really get momentum outside of that small space," Hurt told me. "I wasn't really concerned about how to build a big online brand [at first] and I was surprised when I started to get traction."

The number of page views of Hurt's content increased and a community of people began to show up to read her work and make comments and share her posts. She landed on some "best of" lists and began to get requests to speak and questions about when her first book would be ready.

"It's been a long journey. I've learned a lot along the way. But it was super helpful to have a strategic approach to building the brand." For Hurt, the strategic approach included self-publishing her first book so she would have a story to attract media. This grew the reach of her brand. It also included a consistent commitment to creating valuable content. ☣ "I have been blogging consistently, multiple times a week, since 2012. I blogged for two years before leaving Verizon. We continue because we know that 80 percent of our business comes from content marketing."

Hurt successfully transitioned from a traditional thought leader as an executive at Verizon Wireless to a widely recognized thought leader both online and offline and the owner of a successful training and speaking business. She is often asked to talk about how she achieved this. "A lot of times we'll talk to people and they'll ask what I did. When I tell them I've been blogging since 2012, every week consistently, they tell me they don't want to do that. I think you're the first one that said to me, 'You've got to show up consistently.' And that was really, really good advice."[4]

True Reach Experts

When you have successfully closed the gap between your offline expertise and your online presence, you will have created the possibility for the greatest reach for your book, business, message, or cause. People whose online presence matches their significant offline accomplishments are true reach experts.

Although the line between traditional thought leaders and true experts is not clearly delineated, a few key commitments define true reach expert status.

True reach experts show up consistently online over time and add value with their core topic areas. ⬦ It's not possible to create a podcast with three episodes or a blog with a half a dozen posts and expect to have instant reach. Instead, your online presence requires the same level of commitment that you have made to your offline career. ↻ You obviously won't spend the same amount of time cultivating your online presence as you do contributing to your offline work life, but you do need to show up regularly. The longer you work somewhere, the more likely it is that you will be recognized for your contribution. The same applies online. When you cultivate your online presence with the same long-term view and commitment as you devote to your career, you'll become a true reach expert. ∞

True reach experts maintain a carefully curated, current, and complete online presence. One of the gaps legacy thought leaders might have in their online presence is that information about them online is not curated or well organized and may not be up to date.

Legacy thought leaders who want to obtain true reach expert status will invest in building one website as the center of their online footprint. This website will curate information and resources about their contributions to their field, preferably on a named domain (yourname. com) so that they control and shape the presentation of their thought leadership ideas in a powerful way that is easy to access.

Now It's Your Turn

As you've been reading, you've likely been evaluating your own reach in the world. Which is stronger, your online presence or your offline experience? Where have you invested your energy so far?

Whether you are a beginning beginner as I was in 2009 or a traditional thought leader with decades of contributions offline, you will create the biggest audience and most lasting impact with your work if you choose to close the gap between who you are offline and who you are online by showing up with consistent value on your core topics.

Are you ready to get started?

FOR REFLECTION

This chapter introduced four categories of online presence: beginners, masters of branding, traditional thought leaders, and true reach experts.

- Which group are you in?
- If you aspire to true reach expert status, where do you need to develop?
- If you are a traditional thought leader in the legacy-building generation, what is compelling you to invest in your online presence?
- If you are a member of a younger generation of traditional thought leaders, what concerns do you have about creating your online presence?
- Which story most resonated with you?

Additional Resources

Listen to my conversations with Bev Kaye and Karin Hurt, use an online tool to discover which influence group you are currently part of, and identify next steps to help you increase your influence by closing the gap between your offline accomplishments and your online presence.

chapter 2

What Do You Want to Be Known For?

"Fame or fortune—which do you most want to achieve?" the keynote speaker began. "You have to pick one."

My stomach dropped and I pushed back from my desk, distancing myself from the virtual event on my screen. "You're not going to get both," he continued. "I like to go for fortune. I like to go for money or use the book to make money because then I can use it as a positioning tool. If I've done well making the fortune, I can buy fame."

I leaned forward to reach my keyboard and sent a private message to a friend through Zoom chat: "My answer is neither. I want to make a difference."

While neither fame nor fortune is inherently evil, I recoiled from the speaker's assertions because his comments missed what I believe are the most important reasons creators share content: to create meaning and make a difference.

When I hear people express passionate ambitions about their work, what they say is not typically self-serving. Instead, they speak of a desire to serve others. They see their best ideas as a treasure and want to share that treasure with as many people as possible. For nonfiction authors, books are often deeply personal; they represent the culmination of their life's work. The book is a compilation of their most significant contributions to their fields or an artifact that conveys the core ideas that constitute their legacy.

People in this group want to create greater awareness of the ideas they share because of a deep desire to create value for others. ◈ They want to make their ideas famous more than they want to make themselves famous. They want to create financial success for their work so they can fund more good work. The people they will attract to their work are those who want to join and follow a cause and are not interested in following someone's pursuit of self-interest.

An Author Case Study

Lisa Kohn (lisakohnwrites.com) is one of the authors I've met who is clearly focused on the powerful possibilities for impact her story carries. Kohn says, "I want to spread the message of hope, love, self-compassion, self-love to as many people as I possibly can."[1] Kohn has distilled the message she most wants to share into three points: high-control groups exist everywhere, anyone who feels hopeless or damaged beyond repair can realize that there is hope and they are not damaged, and we all need self-love and compassion. She is committed to providing value through these messages. ◇

I met Kohn in 2013, before she published her memoir, *To the Moon and Back: A Childhood Under the Influence* (2018). Kohn has worked tirelessly to get her message out to people who can benefit from it. Her book tells the story of growing up in a religious cult. She says, "The best seats I ever had at Madison Square Garden were at my mother's wedding. And the best cocaine I ever had was from my father's friend, the judge."

Kohn says she seeks fame and fortune in order to be able to share the message with others: "If I can get famous enough that my story is big enough that other people can be in their situation and know that they have hope, then it's all worth it."

Kohn has learned that spreading her message requires a consistent focus and consistent work and plans to keep sharing the message through her life. She has made a commitment to longevity of work. ↻ ∞

To create a consistent presence, Kohn says yes to almost any opportunity to keep her message going. "Maybe this next opportunity will help my message take off. If I reach that one person who's in pain, then that's why I'm really doing it." ↻

Generosity has been a big part of Kohn's journey: "I am very generous with the book itself, giving away books. If I meet someone in an extreme situation, or born and raised in an extreme situation, I will always give them the book for free, give them an electronic book, or send them a print copy of the book. I try to be generous with my time and generous in sharing my story." She also does a lot of speaking about her book's topics to nonprofit organizations for free. ❤️

Kohn notes that the generosity of others has been hugely helpful in expanding the reach of her message. "I have [had] people introduce me to people. I have [had] people open their homes to have me come and speak to their friends. I've had people sponsor events for me. I will do any book club; I will do anything. So generosity has been given to me. And I try to be generous, as I keep going."

A Nonprofit Case Study

Cheryl Rice founded a movement called You Matter whose core initiative is a yearly event called the You Matter Marathon (youmattermarathon.com). Every year during the You Matter Marathon, Rice invites people to share "You Matter" cards with others to spread kindness, compassion, and gratitude.[2]

The organization's website keeps a running tally of the number of people the simple and powerful act of sharing a card with others has reached worldwide. By 2021, Rice's efforts had led nearly 200,000 people in all 50 US states and 83 countries to share 2 million cards. Rice's big goal is to inspire the sharing of 25 million cards by the end of 2025.

Rice has created a community of people who join her each year to participate in the You Matter Marathon. She calls these people the Yummies. Each year, as Yummies share their passion for the project with others, the reach of the community and its members' efforts grow. She is mobilizing people in schools, health care systems, faith communities, and businesses to participate in sharing kindness with others.

Among the Yummies, Rice is famous; she is their champion, cheerleader, and guide. Like Rice, each of us has the opportunity to create and contribute to our own communities.

Rice has looked for every possible means of getting the word out about this initiative. Her motivation has always been about making a meaningful difference, never about being personally known or benefiting financially. At the program's inception she spent her own money and money given by family members to pay for the printing and shipping of You Matter Cards to marathon participants all over the world. Rice is so driven by this passion project that she has donated much of her time to making it happen and has often prioritized it over marketing her own leadership coaching and speaking business. ♥

Since Rice began, she has hoped for breakout coverage that will propel her work to a level that will reach more people. "The first year we launched the You Matter Marathon I was hoping it would go viral. I wanted to be on Oprah. I still have the vision that this message is vitally important. I want everyone to know about it. What I've learned in my years now with the marathon is that it is more about significance. It's not about fame, it's about significance for me."

Rice describes the significance of her work by reflecting on the way her life changed when someone gave her a You Matter Card. Then, when she gave away her first card to a woman in the grocery store, the woman's reaction changed her life. The recipient of the card "started to weep and said, 'You have no idea what this means to me.' And that changed my life."

Rice's experience of receiving and giving You Matter cards helped her realize that she wanted others to have similar experiences. "I knew at that point, I would go to my grave being the You Matter lady and giving out cards for the rest of my life. Just like when you find a TV show that you love, a book, or a pair of shoes, and you have to share them. I wanted other people to experience what I did."

A Case Study from a Thought Leader

Dan Rockwell (leadershipfreak.blog) started blogging as Leadership Freak in 2009. ∞ Rockwell's community of leadership learners has grown as a result of the more than 4,000 blog posts he has published since then. He currently has more than 500,000 followers, fans, and subscribers. To those people, Rockwell is a rock star and a trusted coach who is as reliable as their morning coffee; he publishes new content every weekday at precisely 6:47 a.m. ⟳

His blogging efforts display all of the Four Commitments needed to achieve reach.

He shares helpful leadership content—value. ◈

He writes daily—consistency. ⟳ Rockwell sees his consistency as the secret to his success with Leadership Freak. He said, "I think one of the reasons Leadership Freak has worked is I am consistent, and people know exactly what to expect. I'm writing something that is the same thing every day on the same topic. And I'm writing consistently."[3]

He's been writing the blog for more than thirteen years—longevity. ∞

He shares his insights for free—generosity. ♥

The Four Commitments have enabled him to reach a growing audience of readers. Rockwell's practice of writing a blog post every weekday is a way for him to create significance by adding value to others. He is not a household name and he is not aiming to break out to massive fame or fortune. Yet his efforts are creating significant meaning for the people who follow him as he contributes to his community in a way that is memorable and long lasting.

His life demonstrates that everyday people can do great work in the world and make a huge impact.

Rockwell gives selflessly of his time. ♥ Consider the amount of time publishing 4,000 blog posts represents. Even if Rockwell can write his posts very quickly, pounding out 300 words in 30 minutes, writing that content represents 2,000 hours, nearly an entire year of 40-hour work weeks. However, writing a post is only one part of the process. Rockwell also sets up his posts online, shares them through social media, responds to comments, and engages with his audience. Rockwell has been giving away the best of his learning day after day and week after week for more than a decade.

Success Depends on the Four Commitments

To make the difference they want to, Kohn, Rice, and Rockwell will need to keep showing up with value, sharing generously over the years, their contributions a steady drumbeat in a noisy world. They will need to continue to share their messages through different channels, seeking supporters who will share their ideas and information about their causes, reaching new audiences over time, and adding value to the audiences they attract. The Four Commitments of value, consistency, longevity, and generosity are evident in all three of these journeys.

Whether you are an author, a blogger, a thought leader, a nonprofit leader, or a champion of a cause, you likely have big ambitions for your book, idea, message, or cause.

You are among the everyday people who can do great work in the world and create great impact.

If you agree that fame and fortune are less important than meaning and impact, you are joining the ranks of the difference makers. You are on a path to first become famous to a few and then to grow your impact over the long haul as you seek to increase the reach of your work.

In June 2021, my company celebrated nine years in business with a virtual celebration. We invited past and present clients, past and present team members, and people in our online communities to join us in celebrating the highlights of our journey so far. Though it felt a bit vulnerable to send out such a broad invitation, the array of faces who joined our Zoom that day and the kind and supportive words they said reinforced what matters most on this journey: the people. Forget fame or fortune; the true riches of this life are the relationships we cultivate. The people I've met along the way, the work we've done together, the moments of connection we've shared—they are the true blessing and what fuels my decision to generously add value consistently over time for as long as I am able.

FOR REFLECTION

In this chapter, I described three people who want to gain traction for messages that matter to them. All are clear about what they want to achieve, who they want to serve, the value they want to bring, and the gifts they offer to others through their growing online presence. They've chosen to make a difference and make meaningful contributions. These motivations outweigh any desire for fame or fortune.

- Which of these individuals' stories resonates most with you?
- How clear are you about the message you want to share?
- Who are the few you want to be famous to?
- Who constitutes your most important audience?
- How do you currently practice generosity?

Additional Resources

Listen to my conversations with Dan Rockwell, Lisa Kohn, and Cheryl Rice; and see an example of one of Rockwell's daily blog posts.

chapter 3

Creating Your Brand

Famous people, like famous organizations, build brand recognition. If you want to create lasting and significant impact through your work while attracting the right audiences, you will need to build your brand.

If you are not already thinking about yourself as a brand, I want to introduce you to this concept.

One author I supported was overwhelmed and flummoxed by marketing lingo. He concluded in a self-deprecating and humorous way that perhaps his brand could be represented by a guy in a dunce cap.

Branding doesn't have to be complicated or confusing. In fact, it's super simple. As you seek to grow influence and recognition for your book, idea, message, or cause online, the brand is you.

Your personal brand already exists. Your personal brand is your authentic self, who you are, all the quirks and characteristics that define you. Your personal brand is *not* an unrealistic projection of who you would like to be. Instead, your personal brand encompasses all of who you are right now: both your strengths and triumphs and your foibles and imperfections.

Branding is honing in on the qualities, values, or beliefs that most differentiate you from others. When you focus on those, you will reveal a brand that is memorable, exciting, and recognizable to others.

As you think about branding, you have choices about what to share and how people get to know you.

If you knew me before you started reading this book, you might associate me with my company, Weaving Influence. In the early days of growing my company, my personal and business brands seemed indistinguishable. Both my website and my Facebook page included my name as part of the company's name, Becky Robinson Weaving Influence, and my photo was part of each header. Over time, as my business grew to include more people, I wanted to ensure that my business had a brand identity separate from my personal brand.

As I've grown my personal brand, I've highlighted some of my likes and dislikes. The content I've shared reinforced my brand identity. I've talked about my love of coffee, the fact that I sometimes eat peanut M&M's for breakfast, my love of running, which books I enjoy, and Lottie, my German Shepherd. I've talked about my team, my clients, and my work. To protect their privacy, I've shared less about my husband and children. People have told me that they see my curly hair and glasses as an important part of my brand identity.

As you seek to create reach, it's important to have clarity about the value you hope to bring. Four steps will help set you up for success as you reach more people over time. They are define, clarify, identify, and commit.

Define What Your Goal Is and Why You Chose It

Chances are, you're reading this book because you want to maximize the impact of your online presence. You want more people to read your book, benefit from your ideas, hire you to speak, or get involved in your cause. I encourage you to

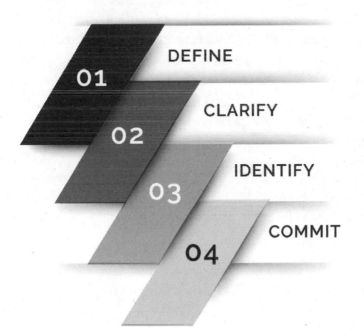

FIGURE 4. The Four Steps of a Branding Strategy

write down your goals and make them as clear and concrete as you can. Decide in advance how you will measure success. How will you know when you've reached your goals?

Mark Miller (markmillerleadership.com), a client of my company for many years, wanted to help as many leaders as possible. "It's always been an aspiration," Miller said, "to reach as many leaders as possible. That's why I'm doing what I do. I feel like I'm on the planet to encourage and equip leaders, and I can't equip anyone I can't reach."

We worked together to both set a goal of how many people to reach and identify ways to measure Mark's reach. He set a goal of reaching 100 million leaders by the year 2030 with his content. Miller knows he can't reach 100 million people through his books, so he looks at all of his work, including his blog, his social media posts, and other free and paid resources he provides. He continues to tweak his approach to measuring reach using a scorecard that combines the reach of each of his various products. In all the things he does, "the ultimate end is to reach people."[1]

Here are some questions to consider as you define your goals for your online presence:

- What do I hope to accomplish?
- What value am I hoping to share with others?
- What do I hope to gain?
- What do I want to learn?
- What am I looking for?
- With whom am I hoping to connect?
- What connections can I help others make?
- How will I measure success?
- What content will I use to express myself? (Writing, photos, art, video, song?)

- What motivates me?
- How strong is my commitment?
- Why do I want to build influence?

Getting clear about the answer to why is important. When you can clearly articulate why you're pursuing reach, you'll be creating fuel to help you persevere on the long journey of creating a long-lasting legacy for your book, idea, message, or cause.

Clarify Your Message

Clear messages gain traction. The clearer you are about the value you bring to the world, the easier it is for people to remember you and the easier it is for you to stay focused on growing traction for your work. ◈

It's easy to remember famous brands because they repeat clear messages through their advertising campaigns.

"America runs on . . ." which coffee chain? Where can you eat fresh? Which paper towel is the "quicker picker upper"? Those simple slogans make it clear what people can expect when they interact with a brand.

What is your area of passion and expertise? If you are already creating and sharing content online, what are you already known for? If you are not creating and sharing content online yet, what are you known for among the people who know and work with you?

If you're having difficulty getting clarity, ask a few friends or colleagues for input. What do they consider you to be an expert about? What is the topic area they feel you are best equipped to talk about?

It may be easy for you to come up with a general topic idea. For example, you may want to be known for helping leaders. Once you have that general idea, dig deeper. What kind of leaders? What do you want to help them be or do? What is unique about the way you help leaders? What is your unique style, approach, or promise to leaders? What personal qualities or personality traits do you bring?

Think about people, brands, or organizations you see as famous. That is likely because they have created "hooks" that help you connect the topic area intellectually or emotionally to the person, organization, brand, or thought leader.

To become memorable, you will need to imprint your unique value in the minds of your people in the communities you want to reach. Do a thought experiment to help you get clarity about your brand-building goal. Think about people you may follow or admire online. Can you quickly articulate the value they bring in a short sentence or two?

Remember, the goal is to create an online presence that will help people quickly and easily remember who you are and the value you can bring to them. ◈ Once you've applied the idea to others you admire, write a short summary outlining who you are and the value you want to bring as a first step toward clarifying your message.

Identify the People You're Showing Up For

If you are just getting started in growing an online presence, identify the people you expect to be interested in your message. These people are often referred to as your target audiences. What kinds of work do they do? What are their job titles or job levels? What is their gender identity? What is their age group? Where do they live? What interests them about your topic? Resist the urge to say that your book, idea, cause, or message is for everyone.

If you are already interacting with people and growing a community of interest around your online presence, what do you know about the people who follow you?

I have gotten to know more about the people who follow and interact with me by inviting interaction with and response to my email newsletters. I send out my newsletter weekly using email marketing software. It's a simple email with my logo at the top. I typically include personal reflection, some links to resources, including information about upcoming events, articles, or podcast episodes, and wrap up my note with a question to my readers, inviting their response. When people reply to my newsletters, I can get to know who they are, what is important to them, and why they are attracted to my work.

What has been surprising is that even though much of my work centers on publishing and marketing books, many people follow me who are not authors or aspiring authors. They work in corporate settings and benefit from the content of the authors my company promotes. To reach both the authors on my list and the leadership learners, I provide a blend of both types of content.

Building online influence is an ongoing process of discovery. You may start with the goal of attracting one kind of audience and learn that other types of people are gravitating toward your work. However, it's still important to begin with an audience in mind and tailor your communication to reach those people.

When you have learned more about your audience, you will have a reason to keep showing up consistently: your community. ↻

Commit to the Long Term

The final step in the process of foundation building is deciding what you are willing to commit to over the long haul. ∞ The Four Commitments of value, consistency, longevity, and generosity will set a foundation for creating the biggest possible reach.

> **Building anything worthwhile is a long-term process.**

You can also commit to actions, approaches, and activities. It's important to commit to a path that will be sustainable for you over time because often you won't see immediate results. Make sure the things you commit to are things you can do over a long period without burning out. So often I see people becoming overwhelmed by trying to do too much or giving up when they don't see quick results. Building anything worthwhile is a long-term process.

The more willing you are to commit to a long-term goal for your online presence, the more likely you will be to find the results you're seeking.

FOR REFLECTION

As you seek to apply the strategies this chapter recommends, answer these questions:

- What personal characteristics are part of your brand?
- Are you comfortable thinking about yourself as a brand? Why or why not?
- Identify the thought leaders you follow. Can you quickly identify the core value or message of their brand?

- What is your most important goal for your online presence?
- Why do you want to build online influence?
- How will you determine when you have reached your goal for your online presence?
- What is your most important message?
- Who is your target audience?
- What are you willing to give to your online audiences?

Additional Resources

Download a resource to explore and clarify your brand, your target audience, and your core message and watch a short webinar about branding.

chapter 4

The Four Commitments

Going Viral Is Not the Goal

When you think about creating massive reach for your book, message, or cause, you may be wondering what it takes to go viral. So many clients have asked me about how to create a viral campaign. Unfortunately, there is no formula for creating content that goes viral. Most often people are surprised when something they do, say, or create becomes viral, and often it's the embarrassing or shameful moments that end up being viewed millions of times.

Viral does not equal value. Most viral content has a very short life. Even if you can create viral content, you will still face the challenge of creating impact over time if you want to make a real difference through that content. For that reason, I don't recommend focusing your energy on creating a viral content.

Instead, start with focusing on creating value. ⬦ When you do that, you may be able to achieve true reach that expands your audience across both geography and time and creates lasting impact.

How Appreciative Inquiry Achieved Reach

I want to introduce you to one thought leader whose ideas have infiltrated almost every segment of society: religious communities, nonprofit organizations, educational systems, and corporations. While it's possible that you know his name, he's not famous. He has not sought fame and fortune. Yet David Cooperrider's (davidcooperrider.com) ideas have caused major reverberations of positive change around the world. His approach to organizational change, a concept he named Appreciative Inquiry, has been used in over 700 books over the last forty years and returns millions of hits in a Google search.[1]

Appreciative Inquiry has been incorporated into

- strategic planning for the United States Navy.
- leadership training for hundreds of international nonprofits in 140 countries, including Save the Children, World Vision International, Catholic Relief Services, the Environmental Law Institute, and The Nature Conservancy.
- keynotes and training by David Cooperrider in fifty-seven countries.

- the United Religions Initiative, which the Dalai Lama and the Episcopal Church in California spearheaded to bring together senior leaders from world religions.
- academic centers at Case Western Reserve University and Champlain College.
- the United Nations Global Compact, a global forum about business as an agent of world benefit.
- major corporations, including Tata Group, Royal Dutch Shell, Microsoft, IBM, Coca-Cola, Starbucks, and Green Mountain Coffee.
- companies that are interested in the B Corporation movement and that follow the principles of conscious capitalism.

David Cooperrider answered an inner call to discover and cultivate a powerful force in human relationships. When he was a junior in college, he traveled by plane for the first time. As he stood in Hiroshima, Japan, looking at the devastation caused by the atomic bomb, he was over-whelmed by the fragility of human relationships and of our planet. But he was also inspired by the power human beings have to shape our world, and he began to consider the meaning of his life and its purpose. He wondered what he could discover that would be "as positive in a human relationship sense as the atomic bomb was in a negative human relationship sense."[2]

As he returned to his studies in social psychology, this question continued to inspire his thinking. When Cooperrider began research at the Cleveland Clinic in 1979, that question infused his approach. When he was asked to do an organizational diagnosis, a common approach that focused on identifying problems and analyzing broken systems and processes, Cooperrider instead found himself in

awe of the innovation, creativity, leadership, and commitment of the staff of the organization that had hired him.
Instead of creating an organizational diagnosis, he "delib-
erately set aside the typical reporting of organizational
breakdowns and instead focused his study on identifying
everything that was giving life, promise, and potential to
the system." He called this "an appreciative inquiry."[3]

Despite his many accomplishments, Cooperrider marks
writing his dissertation as the high point of his career
because of his overwhelming sense that the impact of the
approach could be transformative and wide reaching.

"I felt like this topic wanted to come into the world. It
wasn't just me; it was something that our times were calling for. As it's been said, 'There's nothing more powerful
than an idea whose time has come.' And I felt that, and I
devoted myself to it," Cooperrider says.[4]

As I talked with Cooperrider, all four commitments
of reach emerged as important in the expansion of
Appreciative Inquiry. Beyond these four, Cooperrider made
an important decision that may have been most critical on
his journey to creating impact for his ideas: He decided to
offer his work freely to anyone. While this could be labeled
generosity, it goes beyond that.

He remembers several early conversations about his
work. One was with his mentor, Suresh Srivastva, who
told him that his ideas were going to change the world.
Another advisor, a well-known author and consultant,
told Cooperrider that he had "the tiger by its tail and could
change the field of consulting."[5]

"It was at that point [that] I decided I'm never going
to copyright anything," Cooperrider told me. "Because
this was not my idea alone, it was something that wanted

to come into the world. I made a decision that it's going to grow in creativity, way beyond my imagination, that others are going to bring new approaches and methods to this that I would have never imagined. Instead of a copyright, I have granted anyone the right to copy this. I decided this way before the concept of open-source thinking because it was clear to me [that] Appreciative Inquiry could have a generative impact in the sense of inviting lots and lots of creativity."[6]

Ron Fry, who served as an advisor for Cooperrider's dissertation, was an early collaborator and important contributor to the spread of Appreciative Inquiry. He feels strongly that Cooperrider's wisdom in allowing this work to be available in the public domain contributed to the speed of its spread and adoption.[7] Instead of adopting an exclusive mindset, they approached their work with an inclusive perspective that allowed them to consider how to connect with, share with, and ideate with others. They spent energy and resources expanding their ideas instead of protecting them. ♥

Cooperrider's decision probably increased the impact of the work exponentially. It has been adapted and incorporated by organizational development consultants and practitioners around the world.

Preparing to Implement the Four Commitments

Most of us are unlikely to become monumentally famous in a lasting way. Some people may enjoy fifteen minutes of fame, a momentary flash of publicity. Others may achieve breakout success and create significant traction for their books, messages, ideas, businesses, or causes. It may look like their success has come without much effort or heartache, but that is only because you don't know their backstories. Adding value to the world takes time, effort, and patience. ◈

If you are willing to work hard and if you keep showing up, you'll see results over time. Incorporating the four commitments will help you expand your reach faster and more effectively. These commitments are critical for expanding your audience and creating lasting impact.

Before I dive into the four commitments, I want to share some underlying principles to support your journey of creating reach for your work.

Identify the Right Audience

If you have a great message but focus on an audience that doesn't resonate with your work, you haven't identified the right or complete audience. Changing the focus of your outreach to reach a different audience may result in greater success for your work.

Wendy Ryan (wearekadabra.com), the author of *Learn Lead Lift: How to Think, Act and Inspire Your Way to Greatness* (2021), told me she was surprised by how her book appealed to an audience that was younger than the one she had originally identified. "People four or five years into their careers told me they wished they'd had my book in college," she said.[8] This feedback prompted Ryan to ask business school professors to incorporate her book in their courses.

Getting clear about who the ideal audiences for your work are will help you stay focused on your efforts to reach them.

Resist the temptation to think your work is for everyone. You may think your message or cause is one that may appeal to everyone or is something that everyone needs.

Fauzia Burke (fauziaburke.com) says that while it may be true that many people can benefit from your work, your marketing will be much more effective if you focus on specific communities that have an urgent need for your work.[9] This will ensure that you are reaching people who are ready to hear from you and to receive your work.

Know Your Ideal Audience and Focus on Serving It

Some messages, products, or books have larger audiences than others. You may be able to eliminate frustration regarding your ability to reach people by accurately assessing the potential size of your audience. For example, if you create resources for people with celiac disease, your audience is limited to those people, their close family members, and health care professionals interested in treatment of the disease. Because we know that less than 1 percent of the world's population has celiac disease, you can calculate the absolute largest possible reach for your work.[10] If your work is a book, you can also further narrow your audience to people in those categories who also buy or read nonfiction books.

Gather the Resources You'll Need to Implement the Four Commitments

The reason it feels so difficult to grow reach is that many people lack the resources to create reach. Growing and expanding the reach of your work will take more time, money, and energy than you expect.

Although the spread of Appreciative Inquiry happened quickly, its influence has continued over decades to reach a worldwide audience. You may not be able to replicate its success, but it's helpful to know that dedicated resources will help any idea achieve reach more successfully.

Ron Fry notes that the grants Case Western Reserve University received provided thousands of dollars over many years and an accountability structure that served as an important factor in assuring that research, development, and investment flowed to the implementation and spread of the impact of the concept of Appreciative Inquiry. The value is in both the funds and the structure, Fry says. "With a grant, you have various people that you've brought in under the budget to administer, coordinate, and communicate and as a result there are regular interactions, planning, thinking, and innovating."[11]

If you are fortunate to have access to funding for expanding awareness of your ideas, you're likely to reach farther. More time, energy, and financial resources creates additional reach.

The Four Commitments in Greater Depth

Value

◈ Without a worthwhile book, message, cause, product, or business idea as the basis for your work, it will be difficult to create reach. Starting with a compelling message, an outstanding product, or an amazing book will increase your likelihood of creating massive reach, but it won't guarantee success.

David Cooperrider has said, "The best quality control in the world is to do better work."[12] If the work is good, it will find its audience.

FIGURE 5. The Four Reach Commitments

The best ideas don't always get exponential reach, but an underdeveloped idea will rarely catch on. If you want to create great reach, you need to ensure that what you're offering is something that will attract and retain your audience.

Value starts with you bringing the best of what you have to the world: your knowledge, expertise, point of view, passion, ideas, thoughts, perspectives, and approaches. Whether you are offering a book or message or looking to create reach for a business or nonprofit cause, your audience will decide whether what you're sharing is of value to them.

People may react to the value you're offering online in many ways. See figure 6 to consider a continuum of responses that ranges from "That's not for me" to "That's just what I need right now."

Although some people may see your content but decide that it's not for them, ever, those same people may still see the value of what you're offering and remember it when someone they know could benefit from it. I'm friends on Facebook with a lot of people who may never become authors and as a result would never benefit from the content I share related to strategies for marketing books. Although there may not be value for them, they may remember me when someone they know needs what I am offering. This happens more frequently than you might expect, even from distant connections. My friend Chris Agnoli, who attended church with me nearly two decades ago and with whom I stay connected only on social media, introduced me to an executive in his company as she prepared to launch her first business book.

Some people may be aware of your value and decide it's not for them now. Identifying value is directly related to an individual's interests and needs for their particular stage of life. For example, during the phase of my children's lives when they struggled with bedtime and refused

FIGURE 6. Awareness/Interest Continuum

to nap, I found a lot of value in the work of Elizabeth Pantley (elizabethpantley.com), the author of a series of books that includes *The No-Cry Sleep Solution* (2002). My desire for support in teaching my children to sleep meant that Pantley's work was very valuable at that stage of my life. Now that my children are teenagers, I no longer need Pantley's work, but I would recommend her books and her website to any parents of babies or toddlers.

Others may be aware of the value you offer and follow with mild curiosity and interest, watching from the side-lines until they have a need for what you're offering. I often meet authors who are preparing to launch a book and have come to me with some general awareness of my work because they have known about what I do for months or years but did not have an immediate need to hire me. I recently connected with John Baldoni (johnbaldoni.com), an author of fifteen leadership books. He had been aware of me for nearly a decade but we'd never connected directly. Before Baldoni felt an immediate need for the services I offer, he would have been one of the people who land somewhere in the middle of the awareness/ interest continuum for my work.

On the far right of the continuum of value are people who perceive your work to be of extreme value to them because it meets their immediate need or interest. Most likely, these are the people who will give their support by following your accounts; reading, listening to, or watching your content; buying your book; purchasing your services; donating to your nonprofit; or volunteering in support of your cause. These are ultimately the people you are creating value for; they are your intended audience.

Consistency

↻ Once you start to create and share value with others through your online presence, it's important to add consistency to your approach. Consistency creates memorability because repeating your key ideas and core messages over time helps imprint your unique and valuable ideas and offers in the minds of your followers.

When you are consistent, you demonstrate that people can count on you. Your consistency rewards people's interest in you. When they follow you, they begin to expect the valuable reward of your new content and ideas. Additionally, search engine algorithms reward consistency. Publishing about your key topics over time on your website alerts algorithms to your core areas of expertise and increases the likelihood that people will find you when they use a search engine to look for you or to search for information about your topics.

To ensure that they create value consistently with their content, Karin Hurt and David Dye of Let's Grow Leaders make creating new content one of their most critical weekly activities. "Blogging has become one of our most important things. Even if we have a crazy busy week, even if we're traveling internationally or have 14 virtual programs during the week, we don't not do our blog posts. Doing our blog posts is part of the big rules, because we know content marketing is where 80% of our business comes from," Hurt says.[13]

Chris Brogan (chrisbrogan.com) differentiates between consistency of presence and consistency of action.[14] While some people's influence and reach are greatly boosted by consistency of action, like Dan Rockwell, who has been blogging daily as Leadership Freak for over a decade, or

Karin Hurt, who blogged daily for the first few years of her journey, you can be successful even while you are adjusting to creating new types of content as long as you have a consistent presence. Consistency of action means creating the same type of content again and again. Consistency of presence means creating something to regularly share.

Brogan, who prefers to create different content initiatives and formats over time, relies on consistency of presence. "I quit a lot of things," he admits. "It's fine to decide [that a certain content format] isn't the right way. I think I'll take a different path. Right? What matters is that you're out there producing something, not that you create a streak by creating the same thing 600 times." The end result of creating consistent presence, according to Brogan, is to "be everywhere. Consistency is almost like a visual. When I am consistent, people know where I am."[15]

Putting in consistent effort is critical for creating reach. When you are consistent about creating and adding value, you amass a body of work through your online presence that is credible, valuable, and useful to your online audiences. You become a treasured resource. You make it easy for people to find you. Your core messages come across loud and clear.

Consistency is a commitment. Like Dan Rockwell, you may want to make a very specific commitment to showing up using the same mode of communication on a consistent schedule over time. Or, like Chris Brogan, you may make a general commitment to create and share value by consistently creating something over time even though the form of your communication may change. Either way, it's the consistency of presence, showing up regularly over time, that makes the biggest difference in creating reach.

Longevity

∞ The longer you've been around, the more likely it is that people will see you as someone who offers value through your online presence.

Chris Brogan has been creating valuable content in online spaces since the early 1980s, before the modern internet. When he was growing up in Maine, he started by communicating through bulletin board services. Brogan started blogging in 1998, he began podcasting and creating videos to share online in 2005, and joined Twitter in 2006. The longevity of his online presence contributes to the strength of his network and the reach of his work. The longer you're around, the more people you will reach.

> To create lasting impact, you need to have a lasting presence. The longer you last, the greater the impact you will have.

His longevity also builds credibility related to his topics. When he talks about how to connect meaningfully with online audiences, people listen because he has a depth of experience most people don't have about learning how to use the internet and adapting to and evolving with changes over time on social media.

To create lasting impact, you need to have a lasting presence. The longer you last, the greater the impact you will have.

Brogan warns about the tendency people have to give up too soon. "I did a video where I talked about how it took me 10 years to be an overnight success. That video is almost 10 years old now and is my most viewed video of all time. Ten years later, I'm still working on being an overnight success, and just in new places. Creating reach is a very long process."[16]

The importance of longevity applies regardless of how old you are, no matter when you start. Once you start, keep going. Don't give up. The longer you show up with consistent value, the more your reach will expand and the deeper and more long lasting your impact will be.

Generosity

♥ The commitment to generosity is a commitment to sharing the best of what you have and who you are with others. Showing up consistently over time with an attitude of generosity will contribute to the growth of your reach.

Creating and sharing free content online is in itself an act of generosity. If you know something that can help your ideal audience, share it as often and as widely as you can. Sometimes people worry that giving away their ideas for free will undermine their business success by preventing people from wanting to invest in their book, product, or service. While it may seem counterintuitive, I've noticed that the more generous I am, the more successful my business becomes. The value you provide through generously sharing your expertise creates trust with your potential customers and draws them to you.

Being openhanded and other centered contributes to success in creating reach online. Openhandedness is giving without expecting anything in return. Othercenteredness is thinking about what others need and what might support them best. When you show up to offer value without the expectation of getting anything in return, it disarms people and invites them to receive the value you're sharing.

If you have status, power, or resources, it is important to contribute to elevating the voices of people who lack those things by generously shining a light on their work. You can do this by posting about their work on your social media channels, writing reviews, or making introductions. Be generous not just with people who are similar to you but also with people who don't look, speak, act, or think like you.

Remembering what you have received on your own journey can fuel generosity to others. You would probably not be where you are without the generous support of others who have contributed to your journey by giving you access, visibility, support, encouragement, resources, or opportunity. Generosity is the unexpected element that is common in many people's approaches to building reach for their message, book, or cause.

David Cooperrider's selfless decision to freely share his ideas is one example of how generosity fueled Appreciative Inquiry. Cooperrider also demonstrates generosity through his mentoring of doctoral students, which fuels intergenerational research, and his willingness to co-create new knowledge and explore new avenues with others. His passion for sharing his guidance with students is palpable. "The precious gift that each of the doctoral students brings is what's in them and is wanting to receive full voice. The exciting part of the development in this spread of ideas is the next generation of research and rigorous inquiry, rigorous scholarly reflection, and inquiry," Cooperrider says.[17]

In many ways, generosity has been a key feature in the reach I've had as I've grown my business and online presence. My generosity is fueled by my desire to give what I've so freely received from others.

At the start of the COVID-19 crisis, my team and I started a series of daily webinars to highlight some of our clients' work and to share positive opportunities to connect with our online communities. While it required a significant amount of team time and energy, we saw an amazing opportunity to build relationships with our clients and community members and new connections thrived.

Generosity includes becoming a champion and supporter of other thought leaders, even those who could be considered competitors.

Karin Hurt sees the importance of supporting others. She notes that it starts with remembering that even if people are your competitors, "there is space for everyone. And you need to show up as if these folks are your absolute strategic partners: support their books, support their ideas, as much as you're supporting your own—and it will come back. David and I did a lot of that. When we wrote *Winning Well* people just came out of the woodwork: calling us, offering to help." Hurt says, "I think sometimes people are generous to the people they think will be able to help them as opposed to just showing up generously to help people."[18] Although you may expect that being generous to others will result in people being generous to you, it's also important to be generous to people who may never have anything to give in return.

You Need All Four

Value, consistency, longevity, and generosity are all important as you seek to achieve reach. Without value, you have nothing to offer and no reason for people to pay attention to you. Generosity is the vehicle for delivering value. The more value you give away, the more you draw people's interest and attention. Without consistency, it's difficult to get traction. You may get attention when you launch but fail to create momentum that will help you get beyond your own networks. Without longevity, you may create impact for a moment then fade into obscurity.

Reach comes when you consistently show up with value for a long time and generously share the best of what you have with the world.

> **Reach comes when you consistently show up with value for a long time and generously share the best of what you have with the world.**

Although creating reach takes time and effort, as you share your work with the world, you'll experience joy in learning more about yourself and others and the satisfaction of knowing your work benefits others.

A Commitment to Future Generations

Cooperrider reflected on why becoming a thought leader on social media is important. "We can share ideas in a way of service, giving away ideas that can change lives for the better, institutions for the better, of whole industries for the better. Becoming a thought leader requires a deep commitment to building better worlds. The future is born in our imaginations and minds way before it arrives. We can all influence and work towards articulating the possibilities for better futures. This requires an intergenerational commitment, a commitment to future generations. This commitment opens the world to new possibilities."[19]

FOR REFLECTION

- Which of the four commitments is easiest and most natural for you to incorporate into your work?
- Which commitment do you struggle with the most?
- Which of the three resources of time, energy, and money that you will need to fuel your online presence do you value most right now?
- What new resources could you seek to invest in your work?
- What new possibilities might emerge if you were to focus on a commitment to future generations?

Additional Resources

Listen to my interviews with David Cooperrider, Karin Hurt, and Chris Brogan. Download a color graphic of the four commitments.

chapter 5

The Reach Framework

The Reach Framework provides structure that will help you prioritize strategies for growing your online presence.

Near the center of the Reach Framework are the fundamentals, the first and most critical actions you need to take if you want to build the biggest possible audience and impact for your work over time. The fundamentals consist of your own website, a permission-based email list, content you've created related to your topics (content marketing), and a social media presence.

Neglecting the fundamentals can compromise the effectiveness of other strategies, including public relations. Here's why: journalists or podcasters often evaluate the reach of your online presence to determine whether to offer you an opportunity to place an article in their publication, an interview on their podcast, or a feature on their television show. If your website is out of date or you have little to no social media following, some outlets will choose not to feature you. As a result, the time and money you invest in seeking media attention will not be as successful as you'd like.

What If You're Not Interested in the Fundamentals?

Most people need to tend to the Reach Framework fundamentals first, because they are basic to success in expanding reach. That said, I have met thought leaders who, for various reasons, are not interested in creating a name for themselves or creating an online presence. While I still recommend the fundamentals because they are important to creating the biggest possible reach, other strategies can contribute to expanding reach.

If you have the fundamentals covered or are more interested in investing in actions that go beyond the fundamentals list, chapter 8 will likely meet your needs.

The Reach Framework

The starting point for growing the reach of your message, book, or cause is your website. The center of the Reach Framework has three components: your website, your social media presence, and your permission-based email list. Your website contains all your best content. ◈ It is the place where you regularly share valuable new insights. ⟳ Your social media presence makes new audiences aware of your work and you consistently post value there and seek to build genuine relationships with others.

These basics of the Reach Framework will help you close the influence gap. You will be showing up online with the same value and influence that you create in your offline interactions with people. Showing up online has some basic requirements (a website, a permission-based email list, social media channels) and some optional initiatives (using print, digital, and broadcast media, advertising). The Reach Framework in figure 7 provides an overview of both the basic categories of investment and

FIGURE 7. The Reach Framework

the options you can choose beyond the basics as you work to create reach.

Warning: This can all seem a bit overwhelming. Living out the four commitments of value, consistency, generosity, and longevity requires time, energy, and money. Figure 7 is a visual representation of your path to increasing the reach of your book, idea, message, or cause.

The most important investment you can make online is your own website. Your website is a place where you clearly share the value you offer to the world, where people can very quickly understand your message, and where you can invite people to learn more from you. On your website, you can create and share many types of content to fuel your thought leadership and the growth of your ideas in the world. ◈ This content should be available to your audience on your website. The icons on the home represent the various modes of content you can create, such as articles, videos, or audio content.

> **Any investment you make to create and share content needs to be focused on bringing people back to your domain and onto your email list, where you can communicate directly with them.**

Next to your website at the center, and equally important, is the icon that represents your permission-based email list. Notice the envelope icon next to the house in the framework graphic? That icon represents your email list. One of the important actions you can convince a person who visits your website to take is to share their email address. The circle beyond content marketing is labeled social media channels. Social media is the place to build awareness of your work in order to entice people to learn more about you on your website.

The next ring of the Reach Framework is content marketing. That term refers to the valuable content you create about your areas of expertise in various formats to attract interest and awareness. Chapter 7 provides many suggestions about using the content you create to increase your reach.

Any investment you make to create and share content through digital marketing tools, platforms, or channels needs to be focused on bringing people back to your domain and onto your email list, where you can communicate directly with them.

The Center of Your Reach Campaign: Your Website

Your website is a place you can settle in and carve out a space you own. Ideally, you will be able to purchase a personalized domain name that will make it easy for people to remember how to find you online. In addition, when you own your domain, you have a place you can occupy over the long term. ∞

Your home online is completely yours. You can design it any way you'd like. You own and control it and can update it as often as you'd like. You can build out different rooms and amenities. You can throw open the doors and invite the world in, giving away as much value as you want. ♥ If you prefer, you can open a store. You can do nearly anything you'd like with your online home.

Building a website can take more time and money than you expect. In the same way that your physical home was likely built by professionals, a good website that does all the things you need it to do will likely need the help of a professional web designer. I strongly encourage you to enlist the help of a professional to build your online home.

You may wonder about what the best domain name is for your online home. (A domain name is the URL people type to find your website.) Many authors I meet want to buy their book title as their domain name. If you own a business, you may choose your business name as your core domain name. Or you may want to buy your own name as your domain name, although sometimes it's not possible to do this because someone with the same name has already done so.

One of my longtime clients struggled with deciding how to position his brand and choose a memorable domain name. For many years, he had used the name of his blog as his domain name and established social media accounts using the blog's brand. For various reasons, he chose to shut down that blog and website and had a difficult time choosing a new domain. I had been advising him for some time to use his own name, but unfortunately he could not acquire that domain name. We searched for variations on his name and eventually settled on using one of those.

Don't let the indecision about what domain name to buy hold you up from establishing your own website. You can always change the domain later.

Investing in growing your own website will close the influence gap that occurs when a person's real-life influence is not matched by their online presence. The first step to closing that gap is to create an online home that displays the value of your offline contributions by accurately representing your ideas, achievements, and contributions and the unfolding of your thinking as you continue to advance your work in the world.

If you already have a website, consider whether it is an accurate representation of your real-world value and contribution. Can someone who lands there immediately understand your highest purpose with your work? Can someone quickly identify the resources you are offering? Is a website visitor's next step in engaging with your work obvious and easy to follow? If not, the first step in correcting this influence gap is to revise your website to capture the value of your work more accurately.

The Importance of a Place of Your Own

The internet is a crowded and noisy place. It's constantly changing. New sites, new information, and new platforms for connecting pop up every day. It can be dizzying to sort out how to invest your limited supply of time, energy, and money in a website.

It's easy to get drawn into the allure of growing your influence on well-known platforms. Why invest in building your own website when it seems easier or faster to attract followers and fans on sites where someone else has already done all of the work? People often think it's better to post their content on a site owned by others that is already getting traction, visibility, and reach. While posting on others' sites is a great way to expand your audience, be careful to make sure, at a minimum, that you both retain the content elsewhere and link to it prominently on your own domain. I've written many guest blog posts over the years and failed to retain them. When the owner of the site takes it down, redevelops, or reorganizes, I've lost that value and my ability to share it with others. In order to make sure you retain your content, be sure to keep the articles you've written as Word documents or Google Docs.

While it might seem urgently important to be on all the latest platforms, to stay on the cutting edge of what's new and popular, to reach new people on new platforms, this can be a risky strategy and may result in a lot of effort without a lasting impact. Resist the urge to spend your resources building momentum for a platform that someone else owns and controls.

Your website accurately reflects who you are and the value you offer to others. In addition, it is the place where you can capture, catalog, and create your best content. ◈ People keep their most treasured possessions close to them, in a safe and secure place in their home. In the same way, it's important to safeguard your most valuable content by publishing it on your own website that lives on a domain you own.

Remember, your website is the center of your online presence, your most important asset, the one you own and control. Because of that, you want to be sure people can find and access all the value you offer very quickly when they land at your website.

Should You Have More Than One Website?

You may be wondering whether you should have more than one website to represent the various parts of your work, such as your business, your speaking engagements, your cause, or your books. However, most people need only one website.

To help people see how the metaphor of a website as an online home works, I often ask people how many homes they have. While some people have two or more homes, most people find the expense and upkeep of one home to be enough. Each home you have costs you in property taxes, utilities, landscaping, cleaning, decorating, and more. Each home costs money, time, and energy. The same is true when you own more than one website. Each website requires hosting, security, regular updates, and maintenance. The time required to keep content fresh and updated on more than one website can be overwhelming.

The other challenge related to owning more than one website is the fact that your traffic gets diffused. It takes resources to drive readers to your website. Whether you are investing in support for search engine optimization, relying on search engines as the way people will discover your site, or using paid advertising through social media sites (such as Facebook, Twitter, Instagram, or LinkedIn), a pay-per-click campaign through Google, or free social media to get people to your site, you are spending time and money to create reach for your website(s).

With those expenses and investments in mind, it may still be worthwhile for you to invest in more than one website. For example, if you are building a business or non-profit that you may leave or sell at some point, you will want your own website to be a consistent home for your individual work, something that is separate from your organization. If you have several distinct business entities, they will each need their own websites. In this case, it may be useful for you to have your own name as a domain, an umbrella site from which people can explore and discover your other businesses.

While my most important web property today is weaving-influence.com, I also own and keep beckyrobinson.com current. Though it's unlikely that I'll decide to sell the company I've founded, I will eventually retire or write books that are not related to my company, so it's important to me to create my own brand separate from my company's brand.

If you are an author, you may wonder about creating a stand-alone website for each of your books. In most cases,

I do not recommend this because a one-book website is difficult to keep current, especially when you move on to your next project. Instead, I recommend individual book pages on an author-branded site. You can buy individual web addresses for each book and redirect those URLs to your unique book page. This will enable you to promote those books using a memorable domain name, which keeps all your traffic on your core site.

Here's how it works:

1. You buy a URL specifically for your new book (reachbook.com, for example).

2. You redirect the URL to a page on your primary domain (beckyrobinson.com/books).

3. In your promotions for the book, you use the URL that is easy for people to remember (reachbook.com). You can use it on any print resource related to promoting the book; mention it at in-person speaking engagements, during a podcast, or at a virtual event; and include it in social media posts.

4. When people type the URL in their browser window, they are automatically redirected to the page for the book on your primary site (beckyrobinson.com/books).

Keeping It Current

Content is the container for the value you bring to the world. ⬦

To connect with people regularly, you need to create content that delivers value consistently and over time. ↻ ∞ The content you create becomes a body of work on your website that can instruct, inform, encourage, and inspire people.

> Content is the container for the value you bring to the world.

While you may not be able to write blog content every day, as Dan Rockwell does, it's important to keep your site up to date so the people who find it will see that you're active and present. You will want to be sure you update your site with any new work initiatives in order to keep your online presence in step with your offline activities and influence. You will also want to keep your site up to date technologically with regular backups, updates, and security.

Make Sure You Show Up

Whether you choose to build your online home on a domain that includes your name, a domain name for your business or nonprofit, or a domain name tied to your book title, you will want to make sure that people can get to know you very quickly. In order to reach more people, you need to be relatable. One way of becoming more knowable is to create a friendly and welcoming home page that includes your picture even if you are promoting a business or nonprofit cause. People want to see the faces connected to a business or cause they are learning about. Real photos are easy to identify and create more trust and connection than stock photos do.

The Permission-Based Email List

As you design your website, be sure to focus on the most important action your website can convince visitors to take: giving you permission to send them email. It's important to use your website to draw people to your permission-based list. When people land on your website, make it as easy as possible for them to stay connected to you. Chapter 6 is devoted to a discussion of how to use your permission-based email list to grow your reach.

Using Social Media to Form and Deepen Relationships

Social media is valuable and worthwhile, especially if you view it as a place to find or deepen connections with people. Growing new connections is one of the most important ways to build as you prepare to launch any new initiative.

While your website is your home online, social media channels are any place you go outside your home to meet with or interact with others.

Think of the differences between the relationships you have with people you casually connect with at your favorite corner coffee shop and the closer connections you make with people you invite into your home. In the early years of my business, I would visit a coffee shop after I dropped my kids off at school. The usual people claimed the same tables day after day: Tim, a business owner specializing in background checks who also wrote novels; Shanyn, an accountant; and a few other people whose faces I might recognize but whose names have since faded from my memory. Here's what I can tell you about my connection to those coffee shop acquaintances: We were friendly when we saw each other. The end. I had no way of contacting them beyond showing up at Starbucks and happening to see them.

This, sadly, is the nature of most social media connections. They are surface-level relationships and you have no reliable way of ensuring that you can reach someone when you want to.

Imagine what might have happened if instead of keeping the coffee shop relationships at that casual level I had pursued a deeper connection by exchanging phone numbers or email addresses or inviting the Starbucks customers to come to my home for an evening barbeque. Suddenly, they would have had an entirely different context for relating to me. They would have seen my house and met my husband and kids. I would have been able to reach them directly any time after that.

This is the deepening that occurs when you convince someone who meets you on social media to visit your website. Welcoming someone to your website is like welcoming them into your home. It's important to make it a friendly place and to earn enough trust that your visitors will share their email address with you.

Be Personable So People Can Relate to You

Because social media is a place to find relationships, share content about yourself and be as authentic as possible. This helps people get to know the real you. ⬦

Chris Brogan shares the importance of generosity in social media posting: "Give often and long before you ever have to ask for something for yourself." ♥ He also says, "The best way to use social media is daily, and without needing anything from anyone. That way, people feel like you've been contributing and interacting and supporting all kinds of other people's work long before you need to ask for anything."[1]

If you are a traditional thought leader who has made a significant offline impact, you may be able to accelerate the value of your online presence by connecting with the countless people you've previously worked with or helped in your network. Sabrina Horn (sabrinahorn.com), an entrepreneur who launched a PR firm in Silicon Valley in the early 1990s and then left her company after an acquisition, took some time off from her professional network. "I was essentially off the grid since I left my job in 2018, to spend time with my family. Then COVID hit. The 'grid' as we know it was entirely disrupted. It was during COVID as I was writing my first book, *Make It, Don't Fake It*, that it became really important to get back in the flow and reconnect with people," Horn said.[2]

The massive interest and support from past employees, partners, customers, and colleagues from the days she was leading her firm surprised Horn at several points leading up to her book launch and beyond. Suddenly, Horn's LinkedIn profile, which was dormant during her off-the-grid days, became a lightning rod for her book and an outlet for sharing content during the next chapter of her career.

Relationships Formed on Social Media Can Change Lives

If you're looking to make connections and share value with others well before you need support for your own initiatives or if you are just getting started and taking the long-term view, settle in. Enjoy. Creating relationships through social media can be a fulfilling experience. You may make lifelong friendships, meet future business partners, find helpful collaborators, discover a new passion, or completely transform your life because of your social media interactions and online presence. Or you may share content or build a relationship that radically changes another person's life. ♥

My favorite story of the life-changing impact of social media is about Carrie Koens, who has worked with my company in a variety of capacities since I founded it in 2012. Koens is among the very first people I ever hired. Our business relationship started on Twitter.

I would typically begin my day with the same tweet each time: "Good morning, who's awake?" Then, depending on who replied, I would spend time engaging with and getting to know the people who replied.

One morning in late April, Koens responded and said that she planned to use her day off productively, including sending out résumés. My curiosity kicked in and I asked her what kind of work she was seeking. Her reply: "Dream job: editing (from home) or getting paid to write." After less than you'd expect of the typical hiring due diligence, I hired Koens as an independent contractor for Weaving Influence. She edited and wrote for us. That began a decade-long journey that gave her enough flexibility to accommodate life changes that included adopting five children and pivoting to homeschooling during a global pandemic.

My own life has also changed radically because of social media. After an almost ten-year break from my career during the early years of my children's lives, I started exploring how to return to the workforce. Like Koens, I wanted to work from home and needed flexibility to focus on my growing family. A post on Facebook from a high school acquaintance looking for freelance writers became the beginning of an unexpected way for me to learn about social media marketing and book marketing. These new skills eventually enabled me to found my own company.

Social Media Can Draw People In

Your social media accounts provide important cues to help people decide to get to know you better. People will decide quickly whether you are someone they might want to learn more about. Your posts communicate your brand, what's different about you, including the topics you write about, the attitudes your posts express, and your areas of expertise.

If you don't have social media accounts or if some information is missing or out of date, people will become disinterested. If your profiles appear to be unused (no posts) or abandoned (no recent posts), people may choose not to follow you. A vital, up-to-date social media presence helps people see the value you are bringing through your work.

> **Being consistent with your presence on your chosen channels is more important and more valuable than having profiles everywhere and posting inconsistently.**

I am not saying that you must create and sustain profiles on all the major social media platforms. Instead, think about your desired audience and which channels they are likely to be using regularly. Make those channels your most important priority. Pursue other channels only as you have interest, willingness, and time. Being consistent with your presence on your chosen channels is more important and more valuable than having profiles everywhere and posting inconsistently. ↻

That said, many people are overwhelmed by the prospect of posting regularly on social media channels or they may not enjoy or want to spend their time posting. Creating content in batches and using a scheduling tool can be helpful as long as you commit to a reasonable posting schedule that you can sustain over time. ∞ Be aware that as months and years go by, you may change the *places and formats* where you're showing up, but you will continue to show up in as many places online as you are able to help people connect with the value you're offering. If you need support, you can hire an intern, an administrative assistant, or an agency to support your social media presence. For longer-form content, an editor is a helpful person to have on your team.

A consistent online presence will reinforce your credibility. ↻ "If you go out and do your little marketing campaign and then vanish, you're a bad person, because you're not there," Chris Brogan told me. "You're not part of the community. It feels like you say, 'I'm just here to sell and I'm going to go back to my mountain until the next time I need to eat.' Right? That's how it works. You have to be part of the experience."[3]

Isn't Social Media Enough?

People who are just getting started with an online presence often ask if they can skip building a website and build their social following instead. They may have focused their energy on a particular social media channel, like LinkedIn or Instagram, where they have amassed their greatest traction and following and want to keep growing their online presence on that channel.

While it's encouraging to see the number of followers of individual social media accounts grow, that may not equate to greater reach because you are constantly at the mercy of each platform's algorithms, which determine what content is displayed to the platform's users. The software controls the reach of your content, which can be frustrating and demoralizing.

More than that, you are also subject to temporary outages on platforms and on changes to platforms over time that may limit or change functionality. In the fall of 2021, both Facebook and Instagram went dark during a multi-hour outage. Anyone whose only online presence existed only on those channels also experienced the inconvenience of losing the ability to relate to their audience. Social media profiles are a helpful marketing tool, but they cannot be the only presence you create.

It's normal to have fewer email subscribers than social media followers because there's no easy way for people to sign up to your newsletter through any social media channels. On Instagram, it's especially complicated, because Instagram posts can't include links, so people must first click to your profile before they can get to your link.

What about Going beyond Social Media?

Tapping into networks, securing coverage in print and digital media outlets, investing in paid digital advertising campaigns, and creating virtual and live events can be important parts of the Reach Framework that involve reaching beyond your existing audiences and making connections to audiences cultivated by others. However, it's important to first establish your website, your email list, and your social media networks before investing in these other tactics.

FOR REFLECTION

- Where is your current online home?
- Does it accurately reflect the value you bring to the world?
- How do you feel about using social media platforms to grow your reach?
- What benefits has social media brought to your life?

Additional Resources

Download the Reach Framework graphic in color, watch a webinar about author websites, and download my list of best practices for creating a landing page to market your book.

chapter 6

Your Permission-Based Email List

The Journey and Joys of Building a List

I've been growing a list with varying degrees of effort and intensity since I created my first blog in 2010, before I launched my business. At the time, I had a simple "subscribe for free" form on the left sidebar of the site.

I know from my own experience and from the experiences of many clients I have talked to over the years that growing a list can be a slow process and that it will take time to get the results you're hoping for. What I've seen more than anything is the frustration people experience when they expect that permission to market to someone means that the person will be ready to buy something right away. They expect their lists to lead to sales quickly. When someone opts in, they do so for any number of reasons, only one of which might be to buy from you. When you show up in someone's email and they open your email, you're far more likely to influence them to take action (click a link, buy a product, request a meeting). Although people are more likely to take action based on email than they would be while scrolling a social media feed, there's no guarantee that anyone will buy from you.

When people opt in to your list, they are honoring you with the possibility of interacting with them through their email inbox. Once you've earned that honor, it's up to you to continue to add value in ways that compel that person to stay connected to you or engage with you in other ways.

As our list has grown, one of my greatest joys has been seeing the interaction that happens. It's unpredictable and surprising at times. Not long ago, I had an email from someone I didn't know who mentioned the name of a friend who had referred them to me. The name of the referring friend was also unfamiliar. When I checked our email database, I discovered that the referring friend has been on my email list since 2016.

If you keep showing up consistently and with value for your audience, people will remember you. They will refer others to you. Now that I've been at this for a while, what I've noticed is that eventually you get momentum from your efforts. People may join and stay on your list for years. Then at just the right time, when they or someone they know needs what you do in the world, they'll reach out.

Jon Gordon's Secret to Success

Several years ago, I noticed an announcement of Jon Gordon's (jongordon.com) latest book. I didn't know Gordon well, but I was aware of his brand and his books. Gordon has written twenty-four books, including eleven best sellers, starting with his first publication, *The Energy Bus*, in 2007.[1]

I popped over to Amazon first and saw that his new book ranked around 100 overall on Amazon, evidence of first-day sales that were stronger than any I've seen with first-time authors. I visited Gordon's website and social media channels, expecting to see a big splash about his new book, but I saw very little. I felt very curious about what secret strategy Gordon might have used to create such strong results for his book launch.

Investigating further, I contacted his marketing team. They told me that they had intentionally downplayed the launch of this book because they were planning a much larger launch of a forthcoming title. For this launch, they sent an email to Gordon's highly engaged permission-based list of 100,000 contacts. Daniel Decker, Gordon's marketing manager, told me that "the main thing for Gordon is that we've built his email list to a very strong and engaged list over the years. We give to them weekly with great content. Also helps significantly that Gordon is speaking as much as he is, which is a *lot*. So our pipeline of new followers is constantly growing."[2]

When I met Gordon personally as part of research for this book, he told me that his email list is still the most valuable asset he has in creating reach for his ideas. Six years after I first inquired about Gordon's list, it had grown by 250 percent to over a quarter of a million contacts. These contacts are people Gordon can connect with directly with the value-added content he regularly creates and with announcements of new books.

Gordon's experience demonstrates how building significant reach takes time. His journey to building his engaged email list began in 2002, twenty years ago, before the emergence of email marketing as a thought leadership tool. He began his newsletter as a weekly fax. Like everyone beginning something new, he began with only a few contacts. "Five people initially, then 20, then 100," he told me.[3]

Gordon's consistent practice of sending content to his list over the years has been a crucial factor in his success. It has enabled him to attract and retain a strong following and earn the trust of his communities. ↻ ◈ "Over time, it's consistency, focus, and adding value to people that makes a difference. I share value, people share it with others, and it grows and grows. The newsletter is the best thing—the most important thing—I've done." Gordon's experience demonstrates that showing up consistently contributes to creating reach. "Getting reach doesn't happen overnight but reach exponentially grows over time and you reach more and more people," he says.[4]

As you build reach for your work, your permission-based email list is an important asset.

Why a Permission-Based List Is So Important

If you want to create reach for your book, business, message, or cause, staying in touch easily with the people who are interested in or attracted to your work is critical. People may find you interesting when they see your content online or meet you in person but may quickly forget the value you bring if they do not have a reliable way to stay connected to you.

Never underestimate the gift people are offering when they share their email address with you. Signing up for your email list indicates a willingness to stay connected and an interest in your work. While it's true that people may not open every email you send via email marketing, they are giving you the opportunity to earn their ongoing attention.

If you provide content that is valuable, if you are relatable and helpful, if your content fulfills a need for your subscribers, if your subject lines are interesting and engaging, your followers may open your email. ◇ Once someone does that, you can earn their attention. As people read your messages, you may earn an even deeper connection when they click on a link, buy a product, or, even more significantly, create an ongoing conversation with you.

Chris Brogan is the person whose newsletter I most often recommend as an example of an engaging, helpful, and well-constructed communication tool. What I love about Brogan's newsletter is that when I read it, it feels like he is actually writing to me. I also love that he almost always invites his readers to engage with him by replying, and when I reply, he always answers, usually within moments. What's astounding is that he does that on whatever day I reply, even if I email him on Sunday morning as soon as I receive the newsletter. Brogan has earned the right to my attention and my click-throughs because I trust him to write something worth reading, to be human and authentic, and to be responsive and helpful.

When you have permission to send emails to people's inboxes, you can legally email many people at once. Federal regulations in the United States and country-specific

regulations outside the United States outline legal requirements for sending mass emails. While I cannot advise you
specifically about how to ensure that your outreach follows
these laws, there are some commonsense approaches to
email marketing that I recommend, both because it's the
right thing to do and because your results will be better
when you follow them.

Send mass communications only to people who have
explicitly given you permission. You do not have permission just because you know someone personally, have
emailed them directly, are connected to them on LinkedIn,
or got their business card at an event. Typically, people
give you permission to email them by filling out a form on
your website.

Emailing many people at once is an efficient way to both
add value and make people more aware of your book, business, message, or cause so you can scale the reach of your
work. Without a permission-based list, staying connected
and sharing messages is more time consuming and challenging. It's far more time consuming to send the same
message to each contact individually. The method limits
your ability to scale a message.

What about using social media platforms for sending
content to followers? Reaching people via social media is
not easy. Social media algorithms often change and are
nearly impossible to predict. If you rely on social media
as way of reaching your connections, you will never know
if your important messages have reached them. Because
only a fraction of your followers on social media ever sees
your posts and calls to action, you'll need to repeat them
many times in the hope that more people will eventually
see them. None of the most popular social media platforms

provide an easy way to send bulk messages, and people often regard unsolicited bulk messages on social media as self-promoting spam. You can never be sure that the recipient wants to hear more from you based only on your connection through that platform.

While social media does have value, it's not the value of a direct connection.

Creating a Permission-Based List

If you are just getting started with creating a permission-based list, the simplest way to start is by signing up for an email marketing service such as Mailchimp. Mailchimp includes simple ways for you to create forms that you can share and embed on your website.

Use Your Website to Invite People to Your Email List

You'll want to make sure that the link for joining your list is in a prominent spot on your website. It should be at or near the top of the page. Alternatively, you can use a pop-up to invite people to join. You'll want to make sure you add a form to every page of your website that invites people to subscribe. You want people to see this very quickly when they land on your site.

Create a compelling case for why people might benefit from your communications instead of a making a generic call to action like "Subscribe to my email list." Because nearly every corporate brand and many thought leaders seek your email address for marketing purposes, most people are not motivated to join another list. That is why it's important to describe the value people will receive from you when they receive your emails so they can quickly decide whether your content matches their interests. You can also put a link to your form at the bottom of blog posts or other content you publish so that people who are benefiting from your work can find out how to stay connected with you via email.

While people may not want to sign up for another newsletter, they may be enticed by an offer of free content. A lead magnet is a content resource you offer on your website in exchange for an email address. This can be any content that your desired audience might value, such as an e-book, a white paper, a tip sheet, an assessment, audio content, or video content. People signing up to receive a lead magnet are giving the content creator important information that they are interested in the content. The person receiving the content receives the value of an ongoing connection to the content creator.

A good way to guide people to your lead magnet is a landing page, a stand-alone page on your website that has one specific purpose: gathering a visitor's email address. Sending people to a landing page from a social media post or during a live event focuses their attention on your offer. Once someone arrives there, the only action they can take is to share their email address using your form. The value of having a landing page is that you get information about what percentage of people who land on the page complete the form, which is the same thing as knowing how many people are potentially interested in the content you're creating.

My company often uses social media advertising to attract people to landing pages where they can download our clients' resources. This tactic can be very effective when you want to grow an email list, especially when you've already created interest through social media posts that people who are connected to you find valuable, inter-esting, or entertaining.

While you could and may sometimes choose to give away valuable content without requiring an email address, when you do so, you miss out on the opportunity to create an ongoing relationship with your subscriber. In addition to the value of the free resource, the person sharing their email can stay connected to the content creator and receive more helpful information. The value for the creator of the content is that they can learn who is interested in their work so they can stay in touch.

Of course, once you've created a valuable lead magnet, you'll want to share it with your existing email list. You might wonder why you would send existing subscribers to a land-ing page. Here's why: asking people to sign up to receive a download gives you data about what content your subscrib-ers find value in. That information will give you guidance about creating new content that helps your followers.

Get Permission from Your Existing Contacts to Send Email Related to Your New Project

You may want to reach out personally to people who have been important in your life to let them know that you are starting (or resuming) an email newsletter and to invite them to subscribe by completing the form. Even if you know people really well and even if you're really sure they would want to be on your list, it's important to get explicit permission.

It's possible you have a list of contacts already from your personal or business email communication. However, people you communicate with directly and personally from your email account do not constitute a permission-based list.

> People you communicate with directly and per-
> sonally from your email account do not consti-
> tute a permission-based list.

The same is true for contacts from a previous permission-based list that you haven't stayed in touch with. If you have an existing list, before you start any new marketing initiative, think about how current your list is by noting when you last sent a message to it. If it's been a while since you last emailed your list, it's possible that it has become cold or stale. People may have forgotten that they gave you permission. In this case, it's helpful to write an email that addresses your lapse and outlines what people can expect in the future so they can decide if they'd like to stay connected.

Gather Contacts at In-Person Events

I regularly talk to people who have spoken to tens of thousands of people over their careers both in the United States and in other countries. When I've asked about how they stayed in touch with those people, most admit that they haven't prioritized doing so. When you show up once, people may love you and find great value in your speech. If you have a book, they may buy it and remember you. However, very few people have a presence that is captivating enough to create a lasting impact through a one-time, in-person event.

Jon Gordon told me how he stays connected to people who have attended his live events: "Since the beginning, when I'm on stage, giving a talk, I always offer a way for people to connect even more. The goal is always to stay connected. Because I've spent years traveling and speaking, and have stayed connected to those audiences, I've grown an organic following that is authentic, real, and genuine, made up of people who have seen or heard me speak or read my books."[5] During his speeches, Gordon asks people to visit his website to share their contact information in exchange for a free resource. If you are a speaker who regularly shares your website domain from the stage, it's helpful to have a short, memorable domain name.

Even if you are not a speaker, the important concept here is that creating a deeper connection with people who are interested in your work can help you stay memorable. Gathering email addresses at in-person gatherings is a strategy for growing your list that you should not overlook.

Gather Contacts through Virtual Events

Virtual events are a great way to reach people who are interested in your messages. When people sign up to attend a free virtual event you're offering, you can make sure that it's clear that they are also signing up to stay connected to your list.

It may be challenging to attract people to your events when you don't have a wide network of people following you yet. In that situation, partnering with another more established thought leader can be helpful. If they help promote the event, more people are likely to sign up and attend. Virtual summits often bring together several thought leaders for an event that lasts several hours or even several days. Creating or participating in this type of event can supercharge your list growth.

Other Collaborative Approaches to Growing a List

As you get to know other thought leaders who serve similar audiences, one way to find new subscribers is to partner with others in your space. Our clients have done newsletter exchanges where they share a collaborator's lead magnet in their newsletters and then the other thought leader includes theirs, but the cross-sharing could be even more casual and organic.

Are there other thought leaders whose work you admire? Promoting their work with attribution in your newsletter is a generous way to share their value with others. ♥ Consider doing it even without an even exchange.

When you are doing your best work in your own way, you have no competition. Resist the urge to view others in your space as competitors. While someone might have a message that is similar to yours or an audience that is similar to yours, each of you is contributing value in unique and helpful ways. By viewing others as collaborators and colleagues instead of competitors and by generously sharing their work, you can help expand interest in the topic and increase the reach of all of your efforts.

Overcoming Your Own Resistance

Often clients say to me, "I don't want to send a newsletter because I'm so tired of hearing from my author friends asking me to buy their books." Instead of considering the value they can create for the intended audience for their work, they worry that they will write emails that people view as annoying or spammy. People will gladly open and engage with email they want to receive, including email marketing they've intentionally signed up for.

Think about a problem you've recently struggled with or a challenge you're looking to overcome. Suppose you landed on a website that contained valuable, helpful, and actionable ideas to address your issue. You feel so convinced that you'll gain new insight from this expert that you enter your email address to subscribe to the content.

What is your response when that expert's email comes into your inbox? If you're anything like me, you open it as soon as you receive it. You read it carefully to see if it contains the answers you are looking for. If the email contains links to content that resonates with your area of need, you click it and consume that content. Then you eagerly anticipate the next message.

People will be excited to open email that

- provides helpful advice for a challenge they're facing.
- contains information that improves their life or work.
- answers a question they're asking.
- entertains them in some way.
- feels personal and relatable.
- offers value, including free resources or coupons.
- connects to them personally.
- respects their time by keeping it short and simple.

Give Your Email Recipients a Personal Connection to You

The more personal an email is, the more likely someone is to respond. Since email marketing is one-way communication, the more real you can become to your audience, the more they will want to hear from you. What can you share that will both help people learn and help them get to know you? How can you invite people into an ongoing conversation with you? What question can you ask to invite them to reply?

Whitney Johnson is skillful at offering people a personal connection to her as she shares valuable information through her newsletter each week. She started her newsletter around the time of the launch of her first book, *Dare, Dream, Do* (2012), and is still sending a weekly newsletter nearly a decade later.

"I think the real challenge for me is that when I write, I don't want to be salesy, and I don't want to be blatantly marketing. Somehow those feel like a bad thing. What I am really saying when I say that is I don't want people to feel like I'm using them," Johnson says. "For me, it was a matter of overcoming that and getting to the point where I would say, 'Okay, I have something that I feel like it's important that I want to share.' When I started, I didn't want to do a newsletter that was all about me. I wanted to do something that adds value."[6]

Chris Brogan wrote this advice as part of his regular Sunday newsletter: "From the very moment I start the letter with your name, to the way I talk as if we're midway through a conversation and not at the beginning, building an email is about seeking a response or action. The action I'm seeking today? A reply." At the end of his message, he returned to that initial focus, "So many people end their letters poorly. It leaves the reader not knowing what the sender had intended for them. 'What should I do next?' Never let people feel that. *What I want you to do*: Hit reply, especially if you haven't in quite a while (or ever!), and tell me that you saw this letter. Tell me what you think. Or what you're working on. Or anything. The goal with *this* letter is simple: replies. Please reply and tell me this was useful (or not!)."[7]

When you send email to people who have asked for it, when you send the content they are expecting and hoping for, and when you infuse your own unique personality into each message, they will open it and engage with what you send.

How Email Marketing Increases Reach

Email marketing is the most effective way to reach people with your messages because once you have permission to stay connected to someone, you can be reasonably sure that your email will land in their inbox. Email marketing allows you to scale your communication by sending to hundreds, thousands, or even millions of people at once. Email marketing software also enables you to test and review the performance of your content in helpful ways. You can track how many people open your emails, click links in your emails, or take other actions. You can also get immediate and personal feedback when people reply to your emails.

To Be Most Successful, Create a Consistent and Sustainable Approach

Jon Gordon says that his email list and his newsletters are the most valuable investments in digital marketing he has made. Two commitments that have contributed to Gordon's success are the longevity of his list and the consistency of his messaging. Gordon currently sends several emails each week.

Without staff to support ongoing efforts, solo practitioners are unlikely to be able to sustain an approach that includes multiple emails every week. I would encourage you to choose a pace you can sustain, even if that is only a quarterly newsletter at first, and to deliver that consistently. Once you can sustain a modest pace, you can increase your outreach. It is far better to sustain regular but infrequent email marketing than it is to begin an ambitious pace of weekly or biweekly delivery and then give up when it becomes too much.

FOR REFLECTION

- If you have a permission-based email list, what works well for you?
- Which of the strategies for growing an email list are you interested in trying?
- If you don't have a permission-based list, would you consider starting one? Why or why not?
- Do you read email newsletters? What do you most enjoy about the ones you read?

Additional Resources

See some examples of successful and effective newsletters, download additional tips for getting started with a permission-based list, and sign up for my Friday newsletter.

chapter 7

Content, Your Flexible Asset

The vehicle for the value you offer the world through your online presence is content. ◈ Because people's attention spans are short and fickle, some content that generates great interest initially fizzles out quickly. To create reach, you need to continue to create and share content through a long-lasting presence. ∞

Interacting with creators regularly reminds me how much they care about their message. Yet amid the busyness of your life and work, you may feel overwhelmed about marketing your work. Jim MacQueen, an author and organizational consultant, told me that joining with other authors to talk about his work made him "realize just how important I think my books are or can be in terms of the value that I hope to bring with them." Staying connected to your deep care about making a difference will help you stay consistent, energized, and motivated over time.[1]

Creating Content

Your website is the place for you to share your best content. You can create many types of content, including written texts such as blog posts or articles, video content, audio content (such as podcasts), or interactive content (webinars or courses).

While it's easy to assume that your followers will like the content format you like, it's good to expand your repertoire and deliver content in a variety of forms to attract different audiences because different people prefer various content formats depending on their time availability, interests, or need. An executive may only have time to consume your content through a podcast, listening on their morning commute, while a new mom might only read your quote graphics as she scrolls through Instagram while her baby is sleeping.

> **Don't overthink, just start creating. You can revise later.**

If you are new to creating content, you may not know which type of content you'll most enjoy creating or even what type of content your audience will respond to. Don't overthink, just start creating. You can revise later. Learn as much as you can about your followers' preferences and needs so you can adapt and adjust.

You can experiment to find out what you enjoy and where you get the most traction for your message. To be most successful in spreading your message, you will likely create a variety of content forms over time.

Here are definitions of some of the basic types of content you can create to fuel your online presence:

- Blog posts: Blog posts are typically 400–600 words long, although they can be much longer. They typically live on your website. Some bloggers write daily, while others write weekly or sporadically.

- Microblogs: Microblogging includes publishing very short articles (200 words or fewer) on your own website. The term also describes short social media posts or captions on a platform like Instagram.

- Podcasts: Podcasts consist of audio content that ranges from casual recordings to highly produced shows. They can be shorter than five minutes or as long as an hour. Podcasts are released in episodes on a daily, weekly, monthly, or other planned schedule. Podcasts can be ongoing or series based.

- Videos: Video content can be casual—shot with your phone, for example—or it can be highly produced and edited. The length of video content varies, but top-performing videos are typically shorter.

Capturing and Cataloging Your Content

Even if you're new to creating content online, you may have already created a lot of content offline. One of the first steps on your journey to creating reach is to identify any content you've previously created both online and offline and organize it in a content library. Every article you've written, every video you've created, every podcast you've recorded, any blog posts, curriculum, course materials, newsletters, keynote speeches, webinars, books, or workbooks you've written are part of your portfolio of content.

Content you've created in the past may seem tired or familiar to you. However, as you share it in new formats online, the work will be new to many of the people who follow you online. And because you will be attracting new followers over time, even content previously shared online will be new to your newer followers.

If you're just getting started, you can start your content library and add to it every time you create a new content asset so that you will be able to repurpose and reuse it over time.

Repurposing Content

Your core messages are the raw materials for content creation. Once you've created content assets, they are a flexible resource you can reshape and repurpose over time. You can use content for multiple functions, including sharing additional value with your audience, attracting new connections, and reinforcing your message to followers.

While you can repurpose your content in many ways, it is helpful to focus on three potential approaches. Where you put your focus will depend on what types of content you have as you start the process of repurposing.

- Adapting or expanding a single content asset to create value in multiple formats
- Repurposing a book or other core content asset into several assets
- Bringing many content assets together to form a book

FIGURE 8. Repurposing a Core Content Asset

Ways to Repurpose Your Content

As you think about repurposing content, think about the various ways you can adapt it.

- Longer form to shorter form or shorter form to longer form
- Text to visual or visual to text
- Text to video or video to text
- Audio to text or text to audio
- Text to interactive or interactive to text

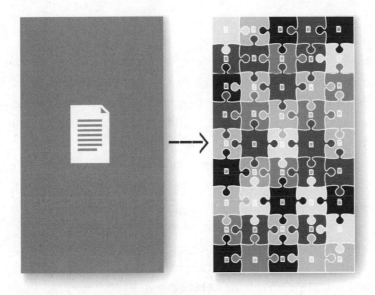

FIGURE 9. One Content Asset Becomes Many

The Value of One Content Asset

Any single content asset can be repurposed and reshaped to create massive value and expand your reach. See figure 8 for a visual representation of this concept.

> **A single content asset can be repurposed and reshaped to create massive value and expand your reach.**

I'll start with a single article. Imagine that I write a 750-word article on the pros and cons of various approaches to publishing: traditional, hybrid, and self-publishing. I create this single asset and publish it on the blog of my website, weavinginfluence.com. (1 asset)

Next, I take the three pro-and-con lists from the article and create a series of graphics, including some key messages from the article, a cover graphic, and a call-to-action graphic, ten in all, to share as a carousel on Instagram. (A carousel is a post on Instagram that includes multiple images, which people can scroll through to read or view.) (1 asset)

Eight of the ten graphics I've created for the carousel will work well as stand-alone social media posts with only slight adjustments. (8 assets)

My communities really enjoy interacting with me through live events, so I plan a webinar on this same topic. I repurpose the Instagram graphics and create a PowerPoint deck to use during the webinar. I deliver the event live, then upload the video to YouTube. I create a pdf from the PowerPoint deck and send that out to the event attendees. (4 assets)

I create a transcript from the recorded video and see that I said some smart stuff. I pull those key quotes and create ten quotes to share on social media. (11 assets)

I pop those ten quotes into the graphic design platform Canva and create some more graphics to share on social media channels. (10 assets)

I decide my podcast listeners might like the content too, so I take the audio file from my webinar, edit out all the chatty stuff from the beginning and end of the webinar, and add my usual podcast intros and outros. (1 asset)

During the webinar, I answered some new questions. I grab those paragraphs from the webinar transcript and write a new article. I publish it as an article on LinkedIn. (1 asset)

I've already created 37 additional assets from the original article.

But there are even more ways to reshape my content!

I use the existing written content, including the graphics, and create an e-book about publishing choices. In it, I link to the podcast episode and the webinar in case people would rather listen or watch. I write a follow-up email sequence (three emails) for people to receive once they've downloaded the e-book. The follow-up sequence of emails invites people to interact with me, ask questions, or share feedback. (4 assets)

I use the pro-and-con list to create an online quiz to help people assess what publishing choice might be right for them. I publish the quiz on my core domain. Once people complete the quiz, my email marketing software will deliver an email containing the results. I include the e-book on publishing choices as a gift in the follow-up sequence (two emails) from the quiz. (3 assets)

I put all the assets: the quiz, the two articles, the e-book, the graphics, the quotes, the podcast episode, and the webinar video into a minicourse. To make the course more robust, I create a list of resources for self-publishing and a list of recommended hybrid publishers. I also record a short introduction video to guide people through the course. (4 assets)

The new total on assets created through this approach, including the original article, is 49.

If you count my using this example in a book, that makes the asset count 50.

And if I pulled together each of these assets and filmed a screen share video to show them to you in demonstrating this process, that would be 51. Fifty-one assets from one article!

You can see the amazing possibilities for reaching more people, in more ways, with more value than one article holds. ◈ You might wonder about the best way to use this content or worry that people will get tired of your content. I don't recommend creating and releasing all of it at once. As you reshape it, you will likely adapt it in subtle ways that will ensure that your content will stay fresh and interesting.

Content is exceedingly flexible and pliable. Reusing your content in different formats on different platforms in different ways will help you reach different people at different times. It will help you create reach.

Repurposing a Book

As you might imagine, a book is an asset that contains limitless possibilities for repurposing and marketing content. A longer-form asset can be repurposed in several ways. The list below uses my book as a model.

A single book of 48,000 words, like this one, could be segmented into articles or blog posts. If each chapter is 4,800 words, with careful editing and some additional content, you could probably create at least three 500-word articles per chapter or thirty articles from the book. (30 assets)

If you retained material from your early drafts that was cut from your final manuscript, you may find a few more articles will emerge from those ideas. (3 assets)

In further distilling the book, using a conservative estimate of five great one-liners per chapter, your book could result in fifty great quotes to share on social media. (50 assets)

Those fifty great quotes could also be made into fifty graphics for social media. (50 assets)

Assuming that each chapter of your book is a stand-alone topic, the ten chapters could become ten webinars. (10 assets)

Those ten webinars could become the core content assets in an on-demand course or live workshop. Or your book could be segmented into ten lower-priced mini-courses. (12 assets)

Suppose that while doing research for your book, you conducted two dozen interviews with experts and recorded your interviews. Provided you got permission from the people you interviewed to reuse the content from the interviews in multiple ways, you could use the audio from each of those twenty-four interviews to create podcast episodes. (24 assets)

If you recorded on video, you could edit segments or highlights into short videos for a playlist on YouTube. If you created two videos from each interview, you'd have forty-eight short videos. (48 assets)

Each of those interviews likely contains powerful quotes that didn't make the cut in your manuscript. If you find two per interview, those powerful quotes can be used as forty-eight stand-alone or text-only social media posts or be transformed into forty-eight graphics for social media. Using the audio recording from interviews, those two quotes per interview can become two audiograms, social media assets that include a snippet of your audio interview. (48 or 96 or 144 assets)

Because you recorded a video, you can also get a transcription of the interviews. With editing, those transcriptions can be turned into question-and-answer blog posts. (24 assets)

If your book focuses on instruction, you can create a course or minicourses online and create live, interactive experiences, both virtual and in person. (2 assets)

If you enjoy speaking, you'll likely be able to identify at least a dozen topics for keynote speeches, either in person or virtual, from your book. (12 assets)

If your book contains reflection questions at the end, you can pull them all together easily to create a discussion guide. (1 asset)

Here's a quick rundown from one book:

- 33 articles
- 50 text-only social media posts
- 50 quote graphics
- 10 webinars
- 10 segments of a course or 10 minicourses
- 24 podcast episodes
- 48 short videos
- 48 text-only social media posts from the interviews
- 48 quote graphics from the interviews
- 48 audiogram assets from the interviews
- 24 question-and-answer blog posts from the interviews
- 1 online, live interactive course
- 1 in-person workshop
- 12 keynote topics
- 1 discussion guide

I have barely begun to outline the possible ways to repurpose the content from a book and I am already at around 350 assets from one book. The possibilities are limitless.

This underscores the extreme value of an asset like a book for fueling online content that shares value with others while it expands the reach of your messages. ⬦

Remember, you can choose what works for you as you repurpose your content. Many of us don't need 350 content assets, even in a whole year. You might be looking at my list above and feeling overwhelmed. I am not prescribing what you must do, I am only describing what you *could* do. If you use even one of the ideas I outlined above to repurpose the value in your book, you'll be multiplying its value and fueling your online presence for months or even years.

Figure 10 illustrates how you can bring together previously created content to form a book.

This is the converse of what I described above. Instead of writing a book and then repurposing it into other formats and content assets, you can start by creating the shorter-form content assets. As you develop your thinking about your core messages, you'll begin to discover a framework for an eventual book. You can create content as you go, testing to see what resonates with your audiences, and when your ideas coalesce, you can pull together previously created content into your book.

You will not be able to copy and paste those assets into a book without doing some significant revision, but your previous content marketing and your other work will be a record of how you explored, expanded, and developed concepts and key ideas.

Although most of the 48,000 words in this book are completely new content, they represent the repurposing of core ideas and topics from my work.

FIGURE 10. Repurposing Content to Create a Book

Repurposing Your Content: A Case Study

Jennifer Bangs (SheBangsSheBangs.com), an actor, musician, and creative from New York City, started out more than a decade ago with the idea of sharing her story of fighting for her marriage as a way of helping others.

Bangs's decision to publicly share her experiences began offline when she started a support group called IGTS (I'm Going Through Shit), a weekly gathering of women experiencing the pain of infidelity in their marriages. Bangs, an avid writer, kept journals over the many years of her marital struggles. She also wrote a memoir but put it aside because of a deep sense that her story was still transforming.

Instead of publishing the memoir, she decided to tell her story through a 75-minute live show. She wrote and produced the show, which included some original music, and performed for audiences in New York City. When COVID forced her to pause her plans to tour the show, she shifted formats and created a series podcast, adding more content. The podcast series—*She Bangs, She Bangs: Marriage, Adultery, Texas, and Jesus*—runs over eight hours.[2]

Bangs's life experiences are the raw material for her content marketing. Her live show is the first asset on her journey. She's recreated and expanded the live show into a twelve-part podcast series. She has plans to reshape it again for a series of YouTube videos. Later, she plans to revise the memoir she wrote to release her ideas in a book.

As I talked with Bangs, we imagined other paths her ideas might take, for example, her vision of a live tour. We also talked about coming full circle with the idea of support groups and how her first idea (IGTS) could become a virtual support group movement to bring women together for support as they fight for their marriages.

Bangs's approach to creating and sharing content clearly demonstrates the value of viewing your creative ideas as flexible assets on your journey to create impact. It's likely that you have one core message or several key messages. Expanding reach is about repackaging and retelling those same messages in different ways over time in order to reach new audiences in new ways. Because you care about your message and about the people you're trying to reach with the message, you take the raw materials of your core messages and bring them to life in new ways over time.

Your core message(s) are the raw materials for your content marketing. Content assets are flexible resources that you can reshape to add value for your audiences. ◈

Repurposing Life

The most important repurposing that happens when you create any content is also what makes your content most unique and compelling. The most important repurposing is the reshaping you make of your life experiences, your hard-won expertise, and your age-acquired wisdom.

Jennifer Bangs chooses to share the raw, painful, messy story of fighting for her marriage through her live show and her podcast. She is unflinching about describing her flaws, her own infidelity, and the ultimate unraveling of her marriage. While many members of her audience appreciate the humor and skill with which she shares her story—the entertainment value—she wants to reach more people so they will experience her work as a source of hope and support.

Bangs is ultimately repurposing more than content, she is repurposing the pain of her life's experience, transforming the broken pieces of her life into something whole and new. If she publishes a book someday, as she intends to, she will be expanding the potential reach of her message beyond the hundreds of people who might attend a live show or the thousands of people who will discover her podcast to include the readers who might benefit from her message.

While your book, idea, message, or cause may not be as closely tied to a personal topic as Bangs's is, each of us can choose to be vulnerable as it relates to our core messages in order to create a powerful connection to our readers. The more real, honest, and accessible we can be, the more likely we are to expand our reach over time.

FOR REFLECTION

- How can you stay connected to your deep passion for your book, business, message, or cause?
- Are you clear about your core messages?
- What is your preferred mode of creating content?
- What content assets have you previously created?
- Which of the approaches to repurposing content fits your situation best?
- What life experiences can you repurpose to give value to others?

Additional Resources

Listen to my interview with Jennifer Bangs, see examples of repurposed content drawn from the examples in this chapter, and download a spreadsheet for cataloging your content library.

chapter 8

Going beyond the Basics

Once you've covered the basics of website, email marketing, content marketing, and social media, you may still feel that you're not creating the traction and reach you'd like for your message. Several possibilities for approaches that will help you create reach for your message go beyond these basics.

This chapter is for everyone who is ready to expand their influence. Whether you've already covered the basics of the Reach Framework or you're ready to jump in to strategies for building legacy, this chapter offers advanced ideas for reaching more people.

FIGURE 11. The Reach Framework

Mobilizing Your Offline Network

While the basic approaches of the Reach Framework position you to reach an expanding online audience, they may inadvertently miss all the people who know and experience your work in real life.

Paying attention to your in-person networks, the people you know offline and who have known you the longest and best, can unlock exponential growth in the reach of your work, especially when those people have been unaware of or unengaged with the messages you're sharing online.

This is why I encourage anyone who is working to build reach online to connect with as many people as possible: friends, colleagues, neighbors, and clients. While that may feel uncomfortable or strange, rekindling lost connections can uncover latent interest and possibilities that you would otherwise miss. When you're launching a project, it's important to give special attention to your personal networks.

> **Every interaction you have is an opportunity to influence and encourage a valuable human being.**

When you do so, remember the important truth that the more personal and specific you are when you interact with people in your networks, the more likely you will be to get a favorable response to your outreach. The people you know in your offline life may not be willing to open and read a mass message.

Reaching out to your offline network is valuable because it deepens your network. Don't overlook the fact that each member of your network is a unique and valuable human, someone you can add value to and whose life you can enrich. Every interaction you have is an opportunity to influence and encourage a valuable human being.

Staying focused on each person's individual worth will help you avoid making network mobilization a self-serving exercise and help you overcome any resistance you might feel about asking people to do things that will support your endeavor.

> We not only need to bring our offline life online,
> we also need to bring our online life offline.

As you reach out to people who have known you primarily offline, it's also important to strengthen online relationships by creating an offline connection. We not only need to bring our offline life online, we also need to bring our online life offline.

What does it mean to bring your online life offline? It means going beyond the superficial following and liking that happens on social media to create a more substantive conversation with people via email, Zoom calls, phone calls, or in-person meetings. No online interaction ever replicates the strengthening of a relationship that comes through real-time, face-to-face interaction.

In the very early days of building online connections, I met a blogger named Tanmay Vora (qaspire.com). He became very memorable to me when he called me from India to wish me a happy birthday. Even though our collaborations over the last decade have been limited, I know he is someone I would support, recommend, and help if he asked and I'm sure he would do the same for me. His action to deepen our relationship by moving it offline demonstrates the value of relationships in our increasingly disconnected world.

Many people loathe the idea of asking people to do things to help them because they don't want to seem needy or exhaust people with requests. It's infinitely easier to ask for help if you've been generous in helping others throughout your journey. ♥ If you start with valuing the relationship and remembering that people will be honored to be asked for help and be included in your work, you may be able to let go of the resistance you're feeling about reaching out to your network to support the launch of your initiative, book, or campaign.

Another note: while you will certainly need the most support when you are launching a new project, involving your network during the entirety of your journey is a helpful way to make asking for help seem more natural, welcome, and expected. In fact, members of your network may be waiting for and anticipating your requests, especially if you have involved them throughout the creation of your latest work.

The value of reaching your networks with your work is that these people represent a much larger potential audience for your work when you consider that each member has their own networks. Each person you can reach with your work is able to reach many others. By involving others in sharing information about your work in the world, you can reach an exponentially larger audience.

The Downside of Focusing on Influencers

Over the years, some of our clients have wanted to focus most of their attention on the most influential people in their networks, giving preference to the people they perceive to have the greatest reach or largest networks. While this can seem to be a strategic and useful way to leverage time and resources, this approach does not guarantee the largest reach for your work. Why? Because people with larger networks likely get many requests for help and your request may be lost in the mix. Additionally, the size of someone's network may be an indication of their reach but not of their engagement with others or their ability to move people to action.

> Never underestimate the power of a regular person to make a difference by sharing your work, especially if they are generous and genuine.

It's impossible to predict which opportunities will create momentum for your work. A person with a small network may wield great influence. These people, who are often called micro-influencers, can have a huge impact. The right word from them about your work at the right time may create momentum and traction for you beyond your expectations. Never underestimate the power of a regular person to make a difference by sharing your work, especially if they are generous and genuine.

Consider Byron Ernest (byronernest.com), an educator from Indiana. Although Ernest has a well-established online presence that includes a solid website and over 200,000 followers on Twitter, he's not a well-known name and may not make anyone's list of top influencers. However, he regularly shares other people's work in his book reviews, blog posts, and other posts. For example, Ernest promoted a book by one of our clients by writing multiple blog posts about the book based on his learnings that week. Excluding Ernest because he's "not influential enough" would be a big mistake.

How to Begin: Make a List

If you are seeking to mobilize your network for the first time, start by making a list of all the potential people in your life to reach out to about your book, message, or cause.

Take your time; you may not think of everyone at once. Don't self-edit and decide in advance that someone will not be interested in your work. Instead, make a list of everyone you can think of.

One way to inspire your thinking is to consider this: if travel, financial, or time constraints were removed and you could throw the biggest party of your life, one to which you'd invite everyone you know or have enjoyed connecting with over the span of your lifetime, who would you invite? If you have previously hosted a large gathering, like a wedding, some of the same people belong on this new list, along with everyone you've met since then.

Either on paper or in an online document like a Google or Excel spreadsheet, create a list of all those people. Remember, don't discount the people who seem to be weaker ties or those you may perceive to have less influence—include everyone on this list. Once you have their names, begin to gather their email addresses or other ways you may have of contacting them, including mailing addresses. If you've had a regular practice of sending holiday cards to friends far and near, your holiday card list may contain the contact information you need.

If you know it, write down the organization they are associated with. You can also create a similar list of organizations that have been important to you along the journey, designating a key contact in the organization who may be able to help you.

What Do You Ask For?

Once your list is complete, add a column for things to ask these people for. You may not be sure what to ask for or how people can help, so it's important to think through these requests in advance. Some obvious asks for almost any endeavor are for people to share your message through their social networks, newsletters, or blogs. If you've

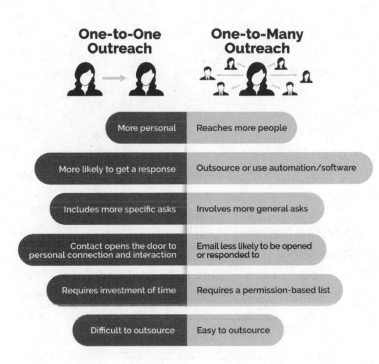

FIGURE 12. Comparison of Types of Contact

written a book, are starting a business, or are launching a nonprofit, you can ask people to host a virtual or live event. Authors may ask for book reviews, business owners may ask for referrals or introductions, and nonprofit leaders may ask for donations. If you have friends who know journalists, podcasters, or others with media platforms, you may want to ask for an introduction to them in the hope that you will gain media coverage for your work.

You may be aware of specific or unique ways the people or organizations on your list may be able to help. When Lisa Z. Fain (centerformentoring.com), coauthor with Lois J. Zachary of *Bridging Differences for Better*

Mentoring, launched her book in early 2020, she had plans to do live events in cities where she'd previously lived and worked. She reached out to a law firm she'd worked with to offer an in-person event based on her book and the firm had committed to buying her book in bulk for the program participants. When these plans imploded due to shutdowns during the COVID-19 crisis, Lisa pivoted to creating online opportunities to share her book with online audiences.[1]

Commit to Personal Outreach with as Many People as You Can

If your list has more than 200 individual contacts, you may not be able or willing to set aside the time to contact all the people on your list individually. Plan how much time you are willing to commit to network outreach and be sure that your plan is realistic given your other commitments. In preparation for the launch of your latest work, you may want to block off parts of days or full days for this important network outreach. Think about how many people you can reach out to and follow up with in the time you've allocated, then highlight that number of names on your spreadsheet. These are the people you've prioritized for one-to-one outreach.

Sabrina Horn created a list of 400 contacts for personalized and individual outreach when she launched her book. Leading up to her June launch, she personally emailed and called many of them and saw powerful results with strong preorders, social media sharing, and book reviews prior to her launch date. Sending mass emails to large groups of people at once would certainly have been easier and less time consuming, but the personal touch was absolutely critical to reconnecting with friends and colleagues and to garnering support for her book.

Cultivate Opportunities with Print and Digital Media Outlets

Landing opportunities for articles, interviews, podcasts or other exposure on media outlets or blogs owned by others can expand the reach of your work to new audiences. These opportunities can be hugely helpful in increasing the reach of your book, idea, message, or cause, particularly if the media outlet has a large audience.

It is important to ensure that you've first invested in building a website and cultivating your presence on social media because media outlets will use your web presence to vet your credibility and value as a contributor or source. Every media opportunity you secure is an opportunity to add value to a new audience and reach new people with the value of your work.

You'll also want to compile (or hire a professional to compile) a press kit. A press kit typically contains your approved short and long bios; promotional copy about your book, product, or cause; and approved photos. These assets make it easy for media professionals to learn more about you as they consider your pitches.

Before you invest in a media campaign, either by contacting media outlets on your own or by contracting with a public relations agency, you will want to ensure that you have clarified the outcomes you're expecting from the campaign and refined the message you want to convey through media opportunities, especially any calls to action.

Some people view mainstream media as the most important strategy for creating reach. While we have seen the major media outlets deliver tremendous credibility for clients, it's important to have a realistic view of what media might be attainable for your work and what results you can expect from media attention once you've landed it.

What Media Is Possible for You?

Nearly every potential client I speak to who is looking for support in gaining media attention mentions Oprah Winfrey's platform as a goal outlet. We all believe that any cause, product, person, book, or idea Oprah endorses will gain mass popularity.

For authors especially, Oprah is a big draw. The *Oprah Winfrey Show*, which ended its 25-season run in 2011, is known for having created the Oprah effect for books. Books that make Oprah's Book Club list become best sellers.[2] However, it is almost impossible for unknown authors to come to Oprah's attention, much less get on her book club list.

Instead of trying to land an opportunity with a major media outlet, it's more realistic to start with modest outlets, build a portfolio of media wins, and look to build media presence from there. Very few business books are featured on national television unless they directly tie to media stories already in progress, for example.

A good strategy is to think about the outlets that speak directly to your audiences. For example, business leadership authors are more likely to be featured in business or trade publications than in mainstream publications. If you're not sure which publications your audience reads, you can do some informal research, for example by asking through a social post or surveying your email newsletter readers.

Sandy Smith (smithpublicity.com), CEO at Smith Publicity, says that most people seeking media opportunities need to build from smaller to bigger media, much like baseball players start in the minor leagues before they make it to the big leagues. Consider the work that a baseball player must do to make it to the World Series. That will give you a more realistic picture of what it takes to land opportunities with national media.[3]

Nearly as important as landing a media opportunity is amplifying the reach of a media win. This is why so many websites showcase the logos of the major media they have appeared on. Although being on the *Today Show* is a big win in the moment, continuing to draw attention to the clip long after the segment has aired builds your credibility and provides ongoing proof about the value of your offer.

When your media win is tied to a book, product, or campaign, the anniversary of a launch can be a good time to repost the original media, since many who are new to your online community may have missed it the first time around.

Media wins can also help you build your online footprint by creating more opportunities for people to find you when they search for you and your core ideas. Press releases also create powerful search engine optimization when they are distributed online by syndication, which includes the publishing of your press release across several high-traffic websites. Syndicated press releases are purchased through a service like PR Newswire.

Digital Advertising

Digital advertising is another way to reach new audiences with your work, although I always recommend maximizing unpaid opportunities to reach people first. Since digital marketing tactics often change, the main idea I want to share here is that targeting ads to your specific audiences can be a helpful approach, especially if your digital advertising approaches lead people to connect with you in a more direct way, for example by attending an online event or joining your permission-based email list. Digital advertising can also be helpful for building awareness of your product, service, campaign, or organization as you launch. One of our nonprofit clients, a community foundation, sees great engagement and awareness when they use social media advertising for their events, especially for the opening date of their yearly scholarship application.

Offer Events

The most powerful spokesperson for your book, message, or cause is you, and the most powerful way to be memorable and engaging is through in-person and virtual face-to-face interactions with people. Every time you show up, you have a chance to increase your reach by giving the people who are present an opportunity to connect with you. The effectiveness of your presence at events is supported by your online presence, so it's important to think about every event strategically to consider how you can connect with people in a lasting way once the event has concluded.

Authors of books in many genres have shared with me how author events have been a critical component of their outreach because meeting and talking to readers has given them a chance to sell their books one at a time while learning more about their readers' interests and needs. While this is certainly not the most scalable approach, it is often meaningful for both authors and readers because it makes the experience of reading and writing more personal.

Whether you are speaking to a conference audience of thousands or interacting one on one with someone interested in your work at a trade show booth, the important thing to consider is how to create an ongoing connection with your audience. The key is always to create enough value and interest that you earn the right to the next connection. ◈ You want the people you meet online and in person to give you permission to stay in touch with them.

> **Ongoing reach is more important than in-the-moment reach because it ensures that you can create lasting impact**

To get that permission, you have to ask for it, so be sure to think through your calls to action in advance of any events. For example, at the end of your keynote speech, you can invite people back to your website to download a free resource related to the content of your event. Or if you're at a local community event, you can ask people to share their email address to receive follow-up information or to receive a relevant resource. The specific details are not as important as finding a way to stay memorable for the people who have just been exposed to your work. Ongoing reach is more important than in-the-moment reach because it ensures that you can create lasting impact.

What would you rather do, deliver a keynote address that intrigues and entertains people for the forty minutes you're on stage or continue to add value to a person who hears your keynote and then continues to learn from and be inspired by your work over time?

Would you rather sell a book to a person at a local event or sell a book to them and later convert the person to a fan who tells others about your work and eagerly waits for your next book release?

Would you rather receive a donation to your nonprofit one time or create an ongoing connection with someone who stays aware of and interested in your cause?

These questions may seem a bit silly, but I have worked with many thought leaders who miss the opportunity to connect in an ongoing way with the people they meet or those who are exposed to their work through events. Of course we would all rather create ongoing relationships for lasting impact, but often we don't think ahead about what is needed to secure that ongoing connection and interest.

In Person or Online?

The COVID crisis put a halt to many opportunities for in-person events and face-to-face interaction. Many people struggled at first to create opportunities to expand the reach of their work. While many are returning to in-person events and interactions, others are continuing to offer online or hybrid events instead. Whether your preference is for in-person or online events, learning to connect with online audiences through virtual events is a critical skill for enhancing your ability to reach people.

Even before the COVID crisis, our team created webinars and virtual celebrations as events that created opportunities for our authors to reach audiences around the world as they launched their books. When virtual events are scheduled to accommodate differences in time zones, they can reach people anywhere in the world. If you are just starting out in gaining an audience online, it can be helpful to partner with others who can invite online audiences to join your events.

More events are better. Letting your network know that you are open to attending events both in person and online is one way to increase the number of invitations you receive. It is also helpful to proactively seek out opportunities to present your work to live audiences. Learn which events are coming up and pitch yourself as a speaker or contributor. Planning your own events works well also.

As with media attention, amplifying your participation in events is key. Talk about each event before and after it happens and share photos from the event. This kind of publicity reminds people of your interest in being a part of events and often results in more invitations.

Always Go Back to the Basics

Remember that investments in media, events, and digital advertising are always preceded by mastering the most important fundamentals of the Reach Framework: developing your own website, updating your online content on a predictable schedule, building your permission-based email list, and sharing content regularly on social media channels. This ensures that any people you reach through these strategies know how to find you and stay connected over time.

FOR REFLECTION

- Which, if any, of these advanced approaches are you interested in pursuing?
- Which, if any, have you tried in the past? What results did you see?
- What media outlets are relevant and realistic for your project?
- What events are you most interested in participating in?

Additional Resources

Download our Network Mobilization Cheat Sheet, download the Go Virtual e-book for creating engaging virtual events, view an example of a press kit, and grab a tip sheet for planning a virtual book-launch party.

chapter 9

Writing a Book to Expand Your Reach

On your journey to get more reach for your idea, message, business, or cause, you may be wondering about whether you should write a book. Maybe you have always dreamed about writing a book but wonder if your book will really matter. You may be wondering about the value a book can bring to you and what the best publishing choice might be for you. Or maybe you've already written a book or several books and you're wondering how they can help you expand your reach.

The Value of a Book

The most successful business book authors become successful by writing more than one book. One book doesn't typically create a big break for an author and make them widely known. They gain additional reach as a result of making a prolific contribution through their writing over time. The cumulative effect of your whole body of work will expand your reach to more and more people. ∞ For fiction authors, a key way to expand the reach of your work is to keep writing more fiction. Historical fiction author Stephanie Landsem told me that the best possible marketing tool for your backlist as a fiction author is your next novel. Many self-published fiction authors release several books in a series at one time to fuel sales and interest.

> A book presents your most important messages and gives readers a road map for your best ideas.

Even one book can be of tremendous value for several obvious reasons and others you may not have considered. A book can bring together your knowledge and experience to establish you as an expert in a particular area. Although the predominance of self-publishing has resulted in a much lower barrier to entry for publishing a book, the time, focus, and intention required to publish at all is a clear sign of your seriousness about contributing ideas on your topic.

A book presents your most important messages and gives readers a road map for your best ideas.

A book can also be a way for followers to get to know you better. A book can grow out of your social media posts to provide a more in-depth way for people to engage with your thinking. A book can be an important way to tell the story of the work your organization is doing in support of a cause.

Becoming an Author

Why do you want to write a book? If you've written one already, what was your motivation?

I've met many aspiring authors over the years. Based on the fact that many of them have told me that they dream of writing a book, I get the impression that it's a universal goal. In 2002 Joseph Epstein claimed in an op-ed piece in the *New York Times* that 80 percent of Americans feel they have a book in them and that they should write it. He titled his piece "Think You Have a Book In You? Think Again."[1]

Here's what he said: "Misjudging one's ability to knock out a book can only be a serious and time-consuming mistake. Save the typing, save the trees, save the high tax on your own vanity. Don't write that book, my advice is, don't even think about it. Keep it inside you, where it belongs."

I want to give you the opposite advice. If you want to write a book, work toward that goal, but do so with your eyes wide open. The truest words I can tell you about writing a book, gleaned from more than a decade of supporting authors, is that writing, publishing, and marketing a book will always take more time, energy, and money than you anticipate.

> You are the only one who can write your book.

Once you know that, if you are still willing to invest what it takes to write a book, do it. Begin to build connections and add value to others, clarify your ideas, and start writing. You are the only one who can write your book, and if you are committed to your message, ideas, or cause, your book will be a tool for expressing your unique value to the world.

Your book does not belong inside you. It belongs on paper and in digital spaces, where it can reach the people who were meant to read it. Let it out.

Even though writing a book is a massive undertaking that has unpredictable results, I still believe that it is absolutely worthwhile to write and market books. Having partnered with hundreds of authors, I also know it's true that a book can deliver opportunities and results beyond your imagination. Most authors I work with learn that the workload is heavier than they expected, but they also experience many wonderful surprises on their journey.

Add patience to your desire to write a book and publish a book. When I started working with authors in 2010, I had already begun to publish some e-books on marketing-related topics. Witnessing other authors' journeys up close fueled my ambition to become an author with an established publisher.

In 2013, an author friend approached me about being a coauthor with him. I agreed, then reconsidered. His book was not my book. Instead, I proposed and outlined another book to coauthor with him, but the project unraveled because of our busy schedules. That same year, I pitched a book idea to my current editor in a face-to-face meeting. I was beaming with possibilities, in awe that I was sitting in a publisher's office suite pitching a book idea. He said no.

In 2015, at an author gathering, a fellow digital-marketing-agency owner who knew that my goal was to write a book one day approached me. He proposed that we create accountability so we could each finish our book proposals. I declined. He wrote his proposal and published his first book in 2016.

Over the years, I pitched book ideas to my current editor at least twice more and got rejected each time.

Busy with building my business, I made peace with the fact that it was not my time to publish traditionally. I wrote more e-books, continued to build my networks, and never let go of my book dream. I view every day since I entered the digital world by joining Facebook in January 2009 as preparation for successfully marketing my book. If you can view your waiting time in the same way, you'll manage the waiting far more effectively.

The book you are reading right now is evidence that my patience and perseverance in waiting for my dream to come true paid off. I expect this book to help expand my reach and to enable me to help more people create lasting value for their books, messages, business, and causes.

Talent acquisition specialist, business owner, author, blogger, and speaker Tim Sackett noted the surprising momentum publishing a book brought to his career: "I thought I'd written so much [on my blog] that I didn't really need a book. And, man, the first year my book launched, it was insane. I had so many requests for keynote speaking and other new opportunities. And I don't understand it fully, but a book takes your thought leadership influence to that next level."[2]

A book is the most powerful way to expand your reach. Even if now is not the right time for you, hold on to your book dream. Even if you hear a no to a proposal, remember that is only a no for now.

You're the Expert about Your Material

If you've been creating content for a long time, you may have previous work that you can reshape to become a book. William Steiner (executivecoachingconcepts.com) wrote *Discover the Joy of Leadership: A Practical Guide to Resolving Your Management Challenges* (2017) by organizing the entries in his extensive blog archive into themes. He wanted to do this so his coaching clients could easily access the writing he had produced during his coaching/consulting career of more than thirty years. His publication gave additional credibility to a business that was already well established. ◈

Chuck Wisner (chuckwisner.com) is writing a book about conscious conversations, a topic he's worked on with Fortune 500 clients for decades. His book will include the core thought leadership ideas and frameworks he's shared with clients through his coaching, training, and writing but has not published widely up until now. ◈

Mark Miller notes that the process of writing a book forces an author to clarify their ideas to make them teachable. He has seen that crafting a book requires that you organize, distill, and illustrate your ideas so they will be more accessible to others. He also has found that writing and publishing a book causes people to listen more intently to what you say: "People give you higher standing, they give you more credibility, they give what you say more validity."[3]

Why Write a Book?

A book is an inexpensive way for readers to experience a closer relationship to people they admire. Reading the book may help them feel that the author is including them in a community.

Alexi Pappas (alexipappas.com) is an Olympic athlete, a representative for Champion sportswear, a filmmaker, an actress, and a spokesperson for mental health causes. She has more than 100,000 followers on Instagram, a community she calls "braveys." Her Instagram followers were the most obvious audience for the memoir she published in 2020. *Bravey* is a personal look at her life experiences so far. Both her semiautobiographical films and her book appeal to people who want to connect and know more about someone they admire.[4]

Books Create Legacy

Richard N. Seaman (rseaman.org) is a business owner who is passionate about multigenerational family businesses as a way of growing and investing in local communities. He champions the idea that an entrepreneur's highest calling is to build their companies to last instead of looking for a quick exit and massive personal wealth. He grew the manufacturing business his father founded from $10 million in annual revenue to $200 million, in the process giving back to his employees, his community, and global causes. Seaman Corporation, which produces industrial fabrics, is now a third-generation business.

Seaman has developed approaches to succession planning, strategic planning, innovation, and human resources. Over time, he began to consider how to share these ideas beyond the people who were his close connections. For many years, he contemplated writing a book. He published *A Vibrant Vision: The Entrepreneurship of Multigenerational Family Business* in 2019. The book tells the inspiring story of his father's founding of the company in 1949 and shares the many challenges Richard faced and the risks he took as he grew the business.

Seaman successfully captured his most important lessons and messages in his book. Like his business, the book will serve future generations, a legacy that will outlast his tenure leading his company and his life on earth. ∞

A Book Can Emerge from Your Ongoing Social Media Writing to Expand the Reach of Your Work

Maggie Smith's (maggiesmithpoet.com) best-selling book *Keep Moving: Notes on Loss, Creativity, and Change* (2020) began as a series of daily notes to herself that she posted on Twitter.

Musician, singer, songwriter, and artist Morgan Harper Nichols (morganharpernichols.com) is another author whose book emerged from her ongoing contributions to social media and her desire to share her journey and art. In 2017, Nichols began crafting poems and illustrations in response to direct messages her Twitter followers sent her. Her goal is to write 1 million poems for 1 million strangers. Her Instagram account, which in 2021 had nearly 2 million followers, includes her original artwork and poetry. She has now published two books that include her art, her poetry, and her stories: *All Along You Were Blooming* (2020) and *How Far You Have Come* (2021).[5]

Ree Drummond (thepioneerwoman.com) started as a food blogger in 2006. She amassed a huge following, which led to the publication of her first cookbook in 2009 and her own daytime TV cooking show in 2011. Creating a book or book series is a natural way for bloggers to package their work.

A Book Supports Your Cause

Justin Miller (careforaids.org) founded CARE for AIDS, a nonprofit focused on providing support for people with AIDS in Africa, in 2007. In 2019, he published *Beyond Blood: Hope and Humanity in the Forgotten Fight against AIDS* with his two African co-founders to tell the story of their work.[6]

Miller says the book is invaluable for his work, especially when he meets people who are not familiar with what CARE for AIDS does. He takes the book with him to every donor meeting because it does a good job of capturing the unique voices and backgrounds of Miller and his co-founders and helps bring the story of their organization's impact to life in compelling ways. Although the book didn't have the reach Miller initially hoped it would, it will be a resource for years to come, an enduring asset that articulates the history and vision of his organization. ∞

In 2006, Scott Harrison (charitywater.org) founded charity: water. His mission is to provide clean water to every person on the planet. Twelve years later, his book *Thirst: A Story of Redemption, Compassion, and a Desire to Bring Clean Water to the World* (2018) made it to the *New York Times* best-seller list and spread the story of his nonprofit organization far and wide. Extending his reach through the book enabled him to succeed in his goal of bringing clean water to as many people as possible. Three years later, in 2021, he had over 1 million followers. Financial support from his broad pool of connections has enabled his charity to partner with local organizations in 29 countries on over 78,000 projects that will bring clean water to over 13 million people.[7]

Selling Books Is Hard

A book can be a powerful tool for expanding the reach of your business, message, or cause, but not unless you leverage it effectively. You'll need to apply the Reach Framework to keep your book visible in the market so it does the job you created it to do. No book is an end in itself, and the work does not end when you have typed the last word.

> **A book can be a powerful tool for expanding the reach of your business, message, or cause, but not unless you leverage it effectively.**

Many authors find the journey of creating a book to be incredibly challenging. Steve Piersanti's article "The 10 Awful Truths about Book Publishing" outlines the stark realities authors face as they seek to create reach for their books.[8] In short: selling books is incredibly difficult, and it gets more difficult every year as more books are published and enter the market.

Mark Miller shared the dissonance he experiences when someone tells him how life-changing his books have been for them. He'll hear profound feedback about the power of his books to change lives and organizations and then wonder why a book that has the potential to change lives and organizations sells only 10,000, 20,000, or 50,000 copies. "It's like we ought to sell millions of books like that, right?"[9]

One way Miller has overcome the challenge of selling books is to remember that books are seeds. Because he wants to see impact from his books, he chooses to give away as many books as he can, aiming for 10 percent of the number he hopes to sell. He estimates that he's given away 100,000 of his various titles over the last twenty years. In this way, he sows the seeds of the ideas in his books so he can reap the impact of the work they do.

Todd Sattersten, a publisher at Bard Press, has analyzed data from over 7,000 business and self-help titles. He found that books that sell at least 10,000 copies in the first year are more likely to sell many more books over their lifetime than books that don't reach that threshold. Sattersten's research suggests that if you can't generate at least 10,000 sales during the first year, your book won't compete well with all the other books that are out there and all the other things that people are paying attention to at any given time.[10]

That said, Sattersten cautions that many authors give up on their books too early. "Too many authors want to walk away from the book too fast. If you stay with the book longer, your return on that investment increases through what your book generates for you and your business."[11] ∞ It is important to be involved in marketing and selling your book proactively over time, especially during the first year after it is published.

> Getting your book out into the world and into . . . many people's hands is how you're going to make the change that you want in the world.
> —Todd Sattersten

Consider this inspiration from Sattersten: "You've done so much work to write the book, now make sure you put just as much love and effort and energy into trying to market and sell the book because that's where you're going to have the impact. Getting your book out into the world and into . . . many people's hands is how you're going to make the change that you want in the world."[12]

FOR REFLECTION

- Do you want to write a book to expand the reach of your business, message, or cause?
- What do you hope to accomplish by writing and publishing a book?
- Writing, publishing, and marketing a book will take more time, energy, and money than you expect. How do you feel about that?
- Your book can be magic, but only if you use it. What are you willing to do to share your book and its message with the world?

Additional Resources

Discover what publishing approach might be right for you by downloading our e-book *Publishing Choices: Know the Pros and Cons for Traditional, Hybrid, and Self-Publishing.* You can also listen to three podcast interviews about the publishing process: a conversation with Trena White, co-founder of Page Two Books; an interview with Todd Sattersten, CEO of Bard Press; and an interview with Kristen Frantz, vice-president of sales and marketing at Berrett-Koehler Publishers.

chapter 10

Reach for Marginalized Voices

In late September 2020, a twelve-year-old girl named Emma Muniz released a children's book.[1] Have you heard of her? I hadn't, but I have heard of her mother Jennifer Lopez, an actress and singer. Ditto for her famous father, Marc Anthony. Muniz's parents' names are known around the world. Because of her parents' fame, Muniz not only published a book but also performed in a Super Bowl halftime show before she turned 13.

The week Muniz released her book, it debuted at number 20 overall in the Amazon rankings of tens of millions of books. A few months later, it was still selling in steady numbers. Emma's connections to famous parents paved a path to mainstream publicity for her book that include an appearance on the *Today Show*; mentions on People.com, MSN.com, Elle.com, Harper's Bazaar; and more. The headlines all contained the phrase "Jennifer Lopez's daughter."

If you're already famous, wealthy, or accomplished or if you have famous, wealthy, or accomplished parents, it's easier for you to create reach for your ideas. You likely have more resources and you likely have access to technology, experiences, capital, networks, and other resources that people from marginalized populations lack.

The events of the summer of 2020, including the murder of George Floyd, raised the level of awareness of systemic racism and its harmful effects on people from marginalized communities.

Racism creates systemic obstacles for authors who are people of color. The hashtag #publishingpaidme became synonymous with racial disparities in publishing in June 2020 when author L. L. McKinney crowdsourced a document where authors revealed how much publishers had paid them in book advances. The document revealed that people of color receive much lower advances than white authors. This movement also highlighted how underrepresented people of color are in publishing as authors and as industry professionals.

A *New York Times* opinion piece titled "Just How White Is the Book Industry?" revealed that although non-Hispanic white people constitute 60 percent of the U.S. population, they had written 89 percent of the books in the *Times*'s 2018 sample. The authors concluded that if you want your book to be published, it helps if you're white.[2]

I am a white woman who was raised by upper-middle-class parents and had access to a postgraduate education early in life; I completed a master's degree by age 24. I have lived most of my adult life with ample financial resources and started my business after spending nearly a decade as a stay-at-home parent who was financially supported by my husband's employment.

I am acutely aware of the advantages of my upbringing and the privilege I've had as I built my business and achieved my dream of becoming a traditionally published author. As I write about the approaches that have worked to create reach for my own work and the work of my clients, I'm aware that I have major blind spots in terms of seeing and understanding the experiences of people from marginalized communities.

I'm also aware of the experiences of people who have plenty of advantages yet still feel challenged as they work to create reach for their work. If the people I work with, who have ample financial and relationship resources, find it challenging to create reach, how much more do people from marginalized communities feel this struggle? What else do they experience?

What can those of us who have privilege do to advocate for and create change that opens up new possibilities for people from marginalized populations? What do we need to understand?

Unpacking the Complexities of What It Means to Be Marginalized

Minal Bopaiah (brevityandwit.com), founder of Brevity & Wit and the author of *Equity: How to Design Organizations Where Everyone Thrives* (2021), helped me understand that many of us have both marginalized and dominant identities. "While I may be marginalized in terms of the color of my skin, and the fact that I'm a woman, I'm cisgender, which is a dominant identity, I'm not trans. I am college educated and have graduate degrees; that is also a dominant identity. I'm in an income bracket that allows me a lot of privilege. I have no physical disabilities, and that allows me to be part of a dominant group," Bopaiah said.[3]

Bopaiah explains that identifying as part of the dominant culture or as part of a marginalized group is complex across different dimensions. It's helpful to raise awareness of the ways we each experience privilege so that we can be aware of the issues others may be facing.

The more marginalized identities a person has, the more obstacles they may face in accessing the resources, relationships, and opportunities required to create reach for their work. Understanding these challenges and being aware of them is the first responsibility people from dominant identities can take on as they seek to undo the systemic racism in our society. Identifying our privilege is another.

It's a Hard Conversation

To tackle this topic, I interviewed several friends from marginalized identity groups: a white woman from the LGBTQ community, a Black woman, an Asian man, and Bopaiah, who is a first-generation Indian woman from immigrant parents. I didn't view any of my interviewees as speaking on behalf of their representative groups. Instead, I came to each conversation wanting to see each person's experience as unique and listening so I could understand the challenges they may have experienced or observed others experiencing as they worked to create reach for their work.

What emerged for me from these conversations is a desire to approach this topic with humility and a desire to learn more from people about their experiences. I can't understand what it's like to be a person of color. I haven't experienced financial hardship or physical or other disabilities. I haven't felt excluded because of my gender or sexual identity.

Because I haven't experienced discrimination, I need to be more open to experiences of others. As my friend Jenn T. Grace (publishyourpurpose.com), an author and publisher at Publish Your Purpose, gently reminded me, "It's easy to dismiss the experiences of people that are not like you."[4]

Barb Roose (barbroose.com), a Black author, speaker, and literary agent, told me about the challenges people from minority groups might face in seeking publication. She told a story of being at a conference where someone said, "Why are we talking about privilege and publishing? There are so many of us trying to get a contract." Although people from dominant identity groups may struggle to secure traditional publishing contracts, we cannot allow our struggle to blind us to the much more difficult barriers people from marginalized groups face. We cannot just assume that it's just hard for everyone. When we do that, we are not taking into account the many advantages we have.[5]

Recognize the Benefits of Your Privilege

Justin Miller recognizes the benefits he had in beginning his work with CARE for AIDS. He could easily access resources, connections, and support as a result of his existing relationships and privilege as the white male who is the son of a wealthy, well-connected executive at one of America's most iconic privately held restaurant chains.

"Absolutely, [my background] gave me a huge head start in a lot of areas in my life, but even in starting an organization," Miller says. "I had the advantage of being immersed in leadership culture, being immersed in a corporate culture. In starting CARE for AIDS, I had access to any knowledge capital that I needed within a pretty short distance; if I needed support on finance, legal, or marketing, I had access to those types of capital. And I had way more access to financial capital starting off, not just with my parents, but with their first-degree relationships with other major donors. There was already a lot of social equity there. There was a lot of trust that allowed these people to financially invest really, really early on, and most of our relationships, if you trace them back far enough, they can almost always go back to someone that's connected to my dad or his employer. When you think about the full implications of that, CARE for AIDS would look very different if we didn't have those things that were available to us."[6]

> **Privilege creates power and with that power comes great responsibility. —Justin Miller**

Miller's list of advantages gives a clear picture of what people from marginalized communities often lack when they work to build a business, write a book, share a message, or promote a cause: knowledge capital in the realms of finance, legal advice, marketing, and leadership; networks of relationships; financial capital; and the trust of and credibility with influential people. Miller says, "It's difficult to list all of these advantages I have had, because it sounds like I didn't have to work hard, and I did! But that's what makes white privilege so difficult to discover and dismantle. It's a hard journey to realize that even though my work hasn't been easy by any means, I have immensely benefited from a head start that very few people have access to."[7]

Privilege creates power and with that power comes great responsibility, Miller says.

Miller has taken a hard look at how people with privilege can understand and use their power. "It's our responsibility to look at how we steward that power. Power isn't inherently bad—we can use the power and privilege we have to make space for and elevate the voices of people who have been historically marginalized and disenfranchised. But that won't ever happen by chance. You can only use your power to elevate marginalized voices if you acknowledge that you have power to begin with and that the power you have as a member of the dominant culture is very likely unearned power. This influences everything we do as an organization: our hiring practices, our selection of vendors, the voices we listen to and learn from, and how we engage communities of color both in the U.S. and in East Africa."[8]

Even if you don't have advantages like the ones Miller described, it's helpful to take stock of the privileges you have as a first step toward understanding and acknowledging the systemic barriers members of marginalized groups encounter. We can't begin to address the issues until we can see them.

Digging Deeper into Obstacles Marginalized People Face

Each of the thought leaders I interviewed noted slightly different obstacles they've experienced due to their marginalized identities. Bopaiah noted the challenge she faced in building an author platform, a term used to describe the author's connections and influence with audiences who might buy their books. The size of an author's platform might be calculated in terms of the number of followers they have on social media, their past success in securing media placements, and the types of connections they have with other authors and with people in the publishing world. In other words, an author's platform is gauged by the size of their reach. That platform is an asset that many traditional publishers use to determine the size of the book deal they will offer an author or whether they will offer a contract at all.

Building a Platform

As Bopaiah began to explore building connections on social media platforms, she experienced virtual stalking by a person known to her family. At the time, LinkedIn users weren't able to block an account. As a result, Bopaiah didn't join social media platforms early. She feels that it's been harder for her to build her platform because of this.

"Even though I have now been on LinkedIn for a while," Bopaiah told me, "I've had less time building a platform than white men who were able to get on in the beginning and weren't worried about being stalked. What publishers and editors are sometimes missing is that this requirement of a digital platform centers on the experience of white men who have nothing to be afraid of online. This is what we're talking about when we talk about systemic oppression and systemic inequality; one is dependent on the other is dependent on the other. This is why there are fewer marginalized voices that are published."[9]

Leticia Gomez of Savvy Literary Services talked with an author for *Publishers Weekly* about "the platform problem" as it relates to securing publishing contracts for authors who are Black, Indigenous, or people of color. She notes

that there are a lot of great books out there "not being published because the author doesn't have a great platform."[10]

The need to create free content of value is another
issue that presents an obstacle for members of marginalized communities. The luxury of creating content without
compensation is one that only people who have already
achieved financial stability can afford.

It is a vicious cycle: marginalized people struggle to
create strong social media platforms and content because
of systemic biases within white-dominated, patriarchal
systems. That prevents them from securing traditional
publishing contracts, and the lack of a book contract prevents them from reaching wider audiences with their work.

Resources

Bopaiah has experienced a barrier to access to traditional
publishing related to financial status. "It seems like you
almost have to be making six figures to be able to get the
book deal and afford the extra publicity and marketing
around the book. That's definitely a barrier of entry for
most of us."[11]

> Whatever resources you enjoy as a member of a
> dominant identity, consider that those resources
> may be ones people from marginalized identi-
> ties lack.

The #publishingpaidme movement also highlighted
the fact that authors who are Black, Indigenous, or people
of color received lower advances for their books and thus
needed to juggle work and writing. In contrast, higher-paid
white authors might have the luxury of stopping other
work to focus solely on their writing. In these cases, the

financial disparities also revealed a disparity in the time and resources people from marginalized populations have as they seek to share their ideas with the world.

Whatever resources you enjoy as a member of a dominant identity, consider that those resources may be ones people from marginalized identities lack.

Relationships

Connections and networking are critical in creating reach. Justin Miller described the astounding power of his father's network. It connected him to a donor base that has enabled him to raise over $25 million since he founded CARE for AIDS. This has supported his ability to reach thousands of HIV-positive individuals and their families in Africa.

Networks have been instrumental in my journey, too. An early LinkedIn connection with author Jesse Lyn Stoner (seapointcenter.com) led her to make several key introductions for me. She told many authors about my new company in the first months after I founded it and introduced me to Whitney Johnson, my first client. From the credibility Stoner's introductions afforded me, I made more connections that enabled me to grow my business and eventually secure a contract to publish a book with Berrett-Koehler Publishers. In the same way that marginalized groups may enter a vicious cycle where systemic biases block their platform growth which hinders their ability to access traditional publishing which limits the reach of their work, my own ease in accessing networks led to opportunities that led to more opportunities, a definite cycle of support and success.

Another vicious cycle for people from marginalized identities starts with lack of access to relationships with people who can open doors to other resources, such as investors, funding, and mentorship. Bopaiah told me what she has learned about accessing traditional publishing: "I have had some really great mentors who have opened up doors. What I realized very late in the game is that it's really much more about relationships and networking than the quality of your work and submitting cold submissions."[12]

Dr. Natalie Nixon (figure8thinking.com), the author of the best-selling book *The Creativity Leap*, described her tumultuous journey to traditional publication and how pivotal her relationships were:

> The experience often seemed a bit absurd. Many times I felt like I was howling in the wind. I didn't have an agent. I sent out book proposals and received rejection after rejection after rejection over a period of 18 months. I began to think thoughts like "Maybe my ideas aren't important. Maybe I should self-publish. Maybe I should make a pamphlet." My husband, my biggest encourager, told me I should keep trying. As a last resort in January of 2019, I emailed about seven people whose work I admire from afar. I knew that they were highly published, so I asked them if they wouldn't mind sharing my proposal among their publishing networks. One of those seven acquaintances introduced me to my (now) editor. And in a span of 11 days, I went from being in the doldrums to securing a book deal. But it shouldn't be that darn hard. I'm overly credentialed and I know I'm really good at what I do. It's so hard to be able to break through an industry that controls the narrative in popular culture, serving as the gatekeeper to determine the ideas that matter.[13]

What Can We Do?

Creating reach for your ideas is challenging, whether you come from a dominant culture or a marginalized one. Many people have intersectional identities, that is, they have multiple marginalized identities that overlap, resulting in even greater disparities in terms of access to and acceptance by dominant groups.

Where we have advantages and privileges, it is important to consider how we can make a difference, both on a micro level by changing our own attitudes and actions and on a more systemic level by working to change the systems of discrimination and oppression in our culture. While addressing systemic issues is outside the scope of this work, many of this book's additional resources address this topic.

Those of us who want to make a difference individually can start by educating ourselves without expecting marginalized people to do the work of educating us. Jenn T. Grace has said that "our job is to really educate ourselves and make sure our intentions are clear. We can't put that burden onto somebody else through our educational process. It's our responsibility to navigate these conversations in a meaningful way that ultimately serves everybody."

We can also look at our networks and seek to connect, learn, and work with people who look different from us and think, believe, and experience life differently than we do.

> The power comes when you can see people who are different from you as people to be admired rather than as people to help.
> —Minal Bopaiah

Bopaiah recommends intentionally seeking out people who are different from us as mentors to expand our understanding and appreciation of differences. She recommends seeking a mentor from a marginalized identity to "flip the power dynamic and help you understand that people who are different from you don't have to be people you help, instead they are people that you could actually learn from." By choosing to be mentored by someone of a marginalized identity, you will move toward appreciating others and treating them as equals. The power comes when you can see people who are different from you as people to be admired rather than as people to help.

Arthur Woods, the co-founder of Mathison and the author of *Hiring for Diversity*, shared the importance of inviting people from marginalized identities to contribute. "Underrepresented communities typically don't have a seat at the table or a voice in the room. Not only does this translate to fewer opportunities, it also means a lack of overall awareness of needs. You can play a role in changing this by intentionally building inroads to communities you don't normally engage to build awareness and start to make connections. You can start to amplify the voices that aren't in the room and help communities get a seat at the table."[14]

Once we appreciate and admire people who are different from us, we will naturally choose to share their work with others, amplify their voices, and create more opportunities for different voices, perspectives, and ideas to be heard and shared. In this way, we can break the vicious cycle of marginalization and instead be part of positive change. This is one more way of expressing generosity through our online presence and influence. ♥

FOR REFLECTION

- What dominant identities do you have?
- Do you have intersecting identities?
- What privileges and benefits do you have as you work to create reach?
- Do the people in your network look and think like you?
- What might you learn if you intentionally chose to develop relationships with people who look different from you and think and experience life differently than you do?

Additional Resources

Listen to my interviews with Minal Bopaiah and Jenn T. Grace. Download a list of diversity, equity, and inclusion resources for further learning.

Reach as Far as Possible

Creating reach for your message, book, or cause is a long-term investment. I hope that reading this book has given you a glimpse of what is possible and has given you a realistic vision of the hard work that is required if you want to make your biggest possible contribution to the world, reaching the largest possible audience you can.

Justin Miller of CARE for AIDS mentioned how important focused, consistent effort has been for his success in spreading his message. ↻ "For us, it has been a very focused and consistent message for the past thirteen years. I wouldn't say that there's been a moment in time where we've had a breakthrough, with national attention on what we're doing. Instead, we have really been just faithfully telling the story of CARE for AIDS through multiple channels."[1]

Miller understands that it's not important for him to be nationally or internationally known and recognized. What matters is the difference he is making among the people who know about, contribute to, and benefit from his cause. By seeking to add value to the people who are most closely connected to his work, he is creating massive meaning and impact.

For Miller, success is less about reaching millions and more about the depth of relationships he and his team are creating with donors, partners, and clients. His focus on relationships has resulted in this "really organic reach that has been developed over time by being consistent and being excellent in our work."[2]

Reflecting on the one-year anniversary of the publication of *One Woman Can Change the World*, which she published in the middle of the pandemic, just after George Floyd's murder, Ronne Rock (ronnerock.com) wrote to her Instagram audience:

> I'm not sure there's ever really a perfect time to publish a book. The odds of any book making it to a best-seller list are rare. The odds of the author earning a living by writing that book are even more elusive. And life goes on, long after the words are printed on pages. New words are written that will never be seen by the masses. . . .
>
> So, why would anyone even want to write a book at all?
>
> This is why. . . .
>
> You become a part of the living breathing story of the reader. You become a part of the answer to prayer, the new way to see, the questions answered, the wondering

and the wandering, the inspiration, the challenge. You help open the door to the next step or opportunity or decision or dream—or the next words.

A writer's work is not validated by the size of the audi-ence, nor is it diminished by the ranking on a best-seller list.[3]

Resources That Contribute to Reach

If you want to expand your audience while making a last-ing impact, you need to start with a decision to add value through the ideas you share, the content you create, and the causes you champion.

You'll need to have a long-term view because creating reach may take a long time, longer than you expect. You'll need a healthy dose of patience.

It will take a lot of consistent effort, more than you plan for. You'll need endurance and perseverance.

It will require resources of time, money, energy, and connections. Because all of these are precious and limited, you'll need to decide and discover what you can do, what you can outsource, and what you must choose to let go of.

It will require sacrifices and generosity, possibly beyond what you might imagine yourself capable of giving. You'll need to remember all you've received from others and give from that abundance.

It will require you to focus on the future, the differ-ence your work can make for both people today and future generations.

If you incorporate the important commitments of value, consistency, longevity, and generosity into your approaches, you'll create the greatest possible reach over time.

This process is challenging for people from a dominant identity. But remember that people who are members of marginalized communities face additional obstacles that you don't. You have a responsibility because of your privilege to seek changes in the world that will elevate the voices of people from diverse communities.

If you are from a marginalized community or have intersecting identities, your voice needs to be heard. I am committed to learning and growing in this area so I can be part of the change we want to see in the world.

The ultimate outcome of your efforts will be the difference your ideas, messages, book, or cause will make in the lives of others, which is often difficult to see. When we plant seeds through our work, we may never see the benefits to others, either because we never meet or connect with them or because they receive that benefit far into the future, when our work is complete or our lives are done.

Five Hundred Trees

At the beginning of the book, I told you about the property on which I live. It is peaceful and private because it is surrounded by trees that the Sitarski family planted and nurtured. They were planning for the future.

The Sitarskis didn't enjoy the benefits of their work right away. As the new owners of the property, my husband and I are now the beneficiaries of their backbreaking labor. We continue to plant more trees. Some of the original trees are dying and we want to continue the legacy and add to what the Sitarskis started.

When you choose to create and share value online, you can never be sure what the outcomes of that choice will be. You won't know whether you will see the benefits in your lifetime. However, you plant with faith that you have value to add.

You do this not to become famous or create financial wealth but because you want to make a difference in the world and create a legacy for future generations. What are you willing to invest to create the reach you are dreaming about?

Reach
Discussion Guide

Now that you've finished the book, I hope you'll consider incorporating some of the ideas to create reach for your work. The following questions will help you reflect on what you've read and identify what's important to you. I'd love to hear about what's been most significant to you. Feel free to reach out to me via email: becky@weavinginfluence.com.

1. Reach = expanding audience + lasting impact. Which of these is most important to you right now? Why?

2. Who is a famous person who has made a significant impact on your life?

3. Who are some people who have made an impact on your life through online content who are not widely known? What do you appreciate about them?

4. Which of the Four Commitments (value, consistency, generosity, longevity) is most challenging for you? Which comes most naturally?

5. What does it mean to you to plant 500 trees?

6. What is the message you are most passionate about sharing with the world?

7. Who are the people most in need of your message right now?

8. What investment have you made in growing your online presence?

9. What does a successful online presence look like for you? What metrics do you use to determine success?

10. Which of the reach fundamentals (creating a website, creating a permission-based email list, maintaining a social media channel) is most challenging to you? Which do you most enjoy?

11. What is your favorite type of content to create?

12. If you had unlimited resources of time, what content would you create?

13. If you had unlimited financial resources, what content would you create?

14. What are your experiences of being the recipient of email marketing? What types of content do you think your potential followers would like to receive via emails from you?

15. In what ways have your networks supported you in creating reach?

16. Have you written a book? If yes, what value did it bring to you?

17. What ideas do you have about creating reach for people with marginalized identities?

Planning a Launch Campaign

At any point as you seek to grow the reach of your book, business, message, or cause, you are in one of four phases on your journey: a building phase, a working phase, a launching phase, or an advancing phase.

Depending on the breadth of your work, you may be launching more than one project at a time. Knowing which phase you are in will help you direct your efforts in the most strategic ways to expand your reach over time. No matter what phase you are in, you need to adopt the mindset that you are *always in the building phase.*

FIGURE 13. The Four Phases of a Launch Campaign

Phase 1: Build and Deepen Connections

No matter how long you have been working to build reach for your project, you will always be in the building phase. There are always more people to reach.

If you are just starting out, remember that everyone starts at the beginning. It's a place with so much potential for discovery and growth.

If you are a traditional thought leader just beginning to build your online presence, you may feel worried about your learning curve related to the things you need to do to be more effective online. These feelings are normal and understandable. Remember that help is always available. Consider finding a mentor or hiring a professional to work with you on this part of your journey.

Even if you already have a strong online presence, there is always room to continue building. You may also encounter plateaus where the growth of your social media channels or email lists seem to stall. Going back to the basics of the building phase can help you break through those plateaus and breathe fresh life into your online presence: building connections and contacts. I refer to your social media fans and followers as connections and people who have given you permission to send content to their email inbox as contacts.

Make More Connections

From the time you start considering a new project, make more connections on social media. The more connections you have, the more people you can reach. Increasing your connections on social media channels has the potential to exponentially increase your reach because you may be able to reach the followers of your followers.

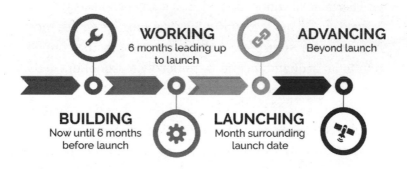

FIGURE 14. Timeline of the Four Phases of a Launch Campaign

It's important to remember that the value to you of various social media channels depends on which audiences you want to reach. A related issue is that the value you receive for your work on any social media channel may change, for example when the algorithms for a channel change so that fewer people are seeing your posts. It's important to pay attention to current advice and best practices about which channel to devote your resources to. No matter what channel you choose, making more connections is an important priority that never ends.

It's also valuable to connect with people whose messages and content resonate with you. As you follow others, you can learn from them, including how they are sharing their messages through social media. You can amplify their content by quoting their work with attribution on your own social media channels. Sharing other people's content on social media is a great way to make connections with them because as you tag them, they'll see your posts. Another way to amplify someone else's content is to provide links to their work when you mention it on your website or in content you send to your permission-based email list.

The value of connecting with as many people as you can is that you can never know which relationships will be most important for your project. An early social media connection to an acquaintance from junior high school opened a door for me to freelance work that later led to the launch of my business. If I had not sent him a friend request on Facebook, I might never have found my current path.

Here's another example. In 2011, while I was promoting a book for a client, I posted a request in a LinkedIn group for bloggers who were willing to write about the author's book. Jesse Lyn Stoner, who was already a published author, responded that she didn't have a blog yet but would be willing to help. I offered to give her guidance about developing a blog and met with her by phone to share some ideas. We developed a friendship, and Jesse later became a strong advocate for my business.

How do you make more connections?

Here are some approaches to try:

- Remember to connect with people on LinkedIn any time you have scheduled a virtual or in-person meeting. You can do this before the meeting if you have their contact information or after the meeting as part of your follow-up.

- Use participation in virtual or in-person events as a way to build many new connections at once. If you attend a virtual conference, the organizers may create networking opportunities or small group discussions. I recommend connecting on LinkedIn with any people you have significant interactions with.

- Use the last few minutes of any in-person or virtual speaking engagement to invite people to follow or connect with you on social media channels.

- Set aside a specific time each week to look for connections with people you know from past and present jobs, neighborhoods, or community organizations. Connect with literally everyone you can think of that you know in real life.

- Proactively follow other thought leaders whose work is relevant to your interests in order to strategically grow your following and to expand your exposure to valuable ideas. This will also give you the opportunity to generously support other thought leaders by re-sharing their content.

Deepen Your Connections

Do you remember running into your favorite teacher in a different setting than school? Perhaps they were with family members at a restaurant or a grocery store. Suddenly, you could see your teacher in an entirely different light.

Seeing your teacher in a different environment added a new dimension to your relationship with them and humanized them. They were no longer just your teacher; after that encounter you saw them more as a whole person with a life outside the classroom.

As adults, we all realize that people are multidimensional, but sometimes we lack the ability to see beyond our limited connections to others. When our interaction is limited to one social media channel, we may have an even more narrow view. You might view a person in a flat way because the easily accessed information about them consists only of an avatar or a profile picture. You may have never clicked on their profile to learn more about their likes and dislikes.

Deepening a connection starts with the intention to relate to others and grow relationships. You can deepen a connection by clicking through to someone's website to learn more about their work or by taking an online relationship offline by scheduling a phone call or an in-person meeting to get to know someone better and to explore possible ways to collaborate.

You can also deepen your relationships with people who have similar interests by learning about and appreciating how they are different from you. The greatest opportunity for you to learn and grow lies in those differences. Cultivate a sense of curiosity and learn from others by asking about their experiences.

Deepening other people's connections with you involves showing up with openness, authenticity, or even vulnerability. While expressing vulnerability may be uncomfortable for you, it can be a powerful way to connect with others. The most effective social media posts are the ones that help people get to know you better—the ones where you show your face, where you show your flaws, where you give people a way to know you as a human being.

Phase 2: Work to Create Assets and Mobilize Your Network

The working phase is the time when you create any assets you need for a successful launch of anything, including both big events, like the launch of your business, a podcast, or a nonprofit cause, and smaller ones, like the launch of a newsletter or an e-book.

A launch is something that you do *with others*. The most important component of any launch is mobilizing others, your network, to participate in your launch. If you're launching a book, your network can help with Amazon reviews. If you're launching a podcast, your network can download and review your podcast. If you're launching a campaign for a nonprofit cause, your network may want to volunteer or participate in telling others about the campaign. It is important to understand how, why, and when to mobilize your network. During the working phase, you will mobilize your networks of connections, contacts, friends, and followers by asking them to join you in creating greater reach for whatever you're launching. Involving your networks so they will tell their networks about your launch can exponentially expand your reach.

This is also the time when you will want to prepare content assets to use during your launch, including social media posts, graphics, blogs, articles, videos, emails, web pages, and any other content your launch requires.

The content you create leading up to launch can be important in building excitement for the launch, creating anticipation for your book, podcast, or event. One author expressed concern to me about revealing too much of his book's content before launch. My experience is that giving people a glimpse of the value to come in your book builds awareness and secures interest. People won't buy your book or product until they know what it is and can see that it will benefit them.

During the working phase, you will also want to schedule and plan for any virtual or in-person events related to the launch and prepare for and plan the details of and logistics for those events. Bringing people together for a virtual or in-person celebration can create enthusiasm about and momentum for your launch.

For the launch of Beverly Kaye's sixth edition of *Love 'Em or Lose 'Em: Getting Good People to Stay,* I hosted a virtual launch party during the evening of her publication date. Friends, fans, colleagues, and family, including Kaye's daughter, brother, and husband, joined a Zoom meeting to celebrate the impact of her work. Special guests, including her publisher, shared the ways the book has helped people in organizations around the world. People Kaye had never met shared stories about her books as important resources in their careers.

Create a Timeline for the Working Phase

The working phase typically begins when you have a launch date in mind for your project. This date is usually set about four to six months before the launch. This is the time to schedule and finalize the details for any launch events so you will be able to maximize attendance and participation. Sharing these dates in advance gives people a chance make room in their schedule for your events.

You'll want to create a timeline that works backward from your intended launch date to ensure that you complete the milestones you need to reach for a successful launch. One important milestone is revising or revamping your web presence or even starting a new website. When I work with clients, I recommend that they complete any changes to their website no later than ninety days before any launch. This gives you time to work through any unexpected challenges and have adequate information about your book, product, campaign, or event ready for visitors to your website.

During the working phase, you'll want to continue focusing on the top priorities of the building phase: increasing and deepening your connections.

Phase 3: The Launch

Sometimes people think of a launch as a discrete event—the launch party, for example. When I use the word *launch*, I am talking about a period of time surrounding the release of a new product, service, book, campaign, or initiative. We typically talk in terms of a launch week or launch month. A launch party or other events can be a part of that launch.

I've met several authors who didn't invest energy in a formal launch of their books. A few months or even a year or so later, they chose to plan and implement a relaunch. This is a valid and helpful approach. If you missed the chance to launch at the beginning of your project, you can always create a launch at a later time. Charles Bergman's book *Every Penguin in the World* launched on March 18, 2020, just as the COVID pandemic hit the United States. As a result, nearly all his planned in-person promotions were canceled. Bergman's book still released on the planned date but without the fanfare he'd originally envisioned. Whether or not something hampers your launch plans, it's always possible to create a relaunch to focus your time and attention on sharing your work with others.

During the launch, you can keep your energy levels high by staying focused on the specific value you are bringing to others. You are not launching because you want to make your own name or enterprise bigger; you are launching because you have something that will benefit others. You are launching *for others*. The larger the reach of your launch, the more people will benefit from your product, service, book, campaign, or idea.

The Basics of a Successful Launch
SCHEDULING LAUNCH EVENTS AND PROJECTS

A launch is something to anticipate. Sending "save the date" messages about an upcoming launch gives you and your communities something to look forward to. You may want to plan marketing messaging with a countdown or other signaling tool. You'll want to repeat your announcements about your upcoming launch in various ways over time because people are busy and may miss your first several messages.

A launch with a specific time frame helps your supporters because it gives them a finite period when you need help. Consider the difference between these two asks related to a campaign:

> "I am working to spread a message about _____. Can you help?"

> "During the month of May, I plan to share a message about _____ with as many people as possible. Would you be willing to share about my project on your social media channels?"

The time specificity of the second request gives people the information they need to determine whether they can make a commitment during a specific time.

If you are launching multiple products or books, give each launch its own season. I supported Mark Miller's book marketing during a period when he launched eight books, all about a year apart. It worked well to give each book its own time to flourish, and planning and executing one launch per year worked well for Mark and his audiences. During those years, Miller also created and offered several companion resources for his books, including field guides, quick-start guides, video series, and assessments, supporting these products by adding them to his website.

Miller notes that many authors and publishers follow the conventional wisdom that releasing a book each year is oversaturation. Instead of seeing a new book as something that has the potential to take sales away from a previous release, Miller believes that releasing new resources fuels interest in his backlist, leading to overall increase of his reach. "Maybe it's that new content that's going to serve a new segment of the market," Miller said.

What has worked well for me and my clients is to pay attention to our own energy. Ensure that any investment you make in creating and launching new products is sustainable over time. If you have multiple book or product releases in a short time frame, make sure that each one enhances your ability to serve new audiences. Otherwise, you can easily burn out yourself and your audience.

Launch Activities
MAKE ONE DAY SPECIAL

Even if you plan a month or a week to launch your product, service, book, or campaign, select one launch day and make the day extra special through an in-person or virtual event and increased messaging or calls to action for that day. If you're launching a book, the publication date is the obvious launch day. This is the day your book is available on Amazon and other online retailers.

If you are launching a campaign tied to a cause or nonprofit, it's helpful to choose a day that already has traction and excitement surrounding it. For example, you can kick off a fund-raising campaign to align with Giving Tuesday, the Tuesday after Thanksgiving. Or you could plan the launch of an environmental cause on Earth Day. There are so many notable days to choose from and choosing a day that is already widely known will give people an anchor for your campaign.

MAKE YOUR REQUESTS CLEAR

For a book launch, there is a very obvious primary call to action: buy the book. While you may feel reluctant to ask people to buy your book, early robust sales create momentum and exposure for your title. Your launch is the one time it's critical to overcome your reluctance and shamelessly ask for the sale.

This is true for any other launch. If you are launching, it's for a purpose. You want to make sure you fulfill your purpose and the way to do that is by making the most important asks.

If you are launching a campaign, make sure the call to action for your campaign is clear. Are you raising money? If so, the call to action is to give. Are you raising awareness for a message or cause? If so, the call to action is to share content. If you're launching a new podcast, the call to action is listen, download, and share.

CELEBRATE

Some people are so focused on the preparation for the launch that they miss the importance of celebrating. A launch represents a culmination of work. If you've written a book, you've put many hours of work into writing it and preparing for the launch. If you've planned a campaign to spread a message or fuel a nonprofit organization, you've devoted many hours to your cause. Any launch deserves a celebration, a moment to pause from hard work to appreciate and enjoy an important milestone.

It's important and helpful to capture the excitement of any in-person launch experiences or celebrations through your online presence. Create a live video or share video footage after the fact. Hire a photographer and take photos of your celebrations. If you are hosting a virtual event, assign someone to take screen captures of your virtual guests. Share those widely, as long as you have permission to do so.

I attended an unforgettable book launch party in San Francisco for Dan Olsen's book *The Lean Product Playbook* in 2015. It was a beautiful evening with great people, great food, and great wine. Dan's family and friends packed into a friend's apartment and spilled outside onto a balcony. The amazing photos from the party photographer that pop up on my Facebook memories year after year are what make this event so memorable. Your party can help you keep your book in the conversation and in people's minds if you choose to share images from it, tag the people who appear in the photos, and revisit the celebration each year on the anniversary of the launch.

Expected Outcomes for a Launch

A launch is only the starting point of a longer journey of creating lasting impact for your book, business, message, or cause. Some launches create massive impact and momentum and others start slowly or are even nonstarters. When your launch creates disappointing results, it is not the end of the story. You can choose to launch again or choose to move on to a longer-term approach to creating reach for your endeavor.

The main goal for any launch is to create as much awareness, action, and reach as possible during a specific period of time. However, be aware that early returns do not necessarily predict the longer-term impact of your launch activities. You might not reach your goals for the launch during the week or month you devote to it, such as selling X number of books or raising X amount of money. I've worked with authors whose early results could have led them to assume that their book had little impact on their bigger-picture goals of building thought leadership or driving additional revenue. However, as the weeks and months went on, those initial investments in launch began to come together and they began to see the actual impact of their launch.

You may be wondering about the value of hiring a publicist to secure media attention for your launch. Investing in media during a launch and beyond can have ongoing value in creating reach. While a launch is not in itself newsworthy, the message of your book or cause may be of interest to media outlets. Placing articles and interviews through online media outlets, including blogs, publication, or podcasts, will give you multiple opportunities to create reach to more readers: at the time the piece is published, any time you share a link to the piece with your online communities, and when your media wins create enhanced search engine rankings for your brand, book, or cause.

Phase 4: Advancing by Developing Further Reach

Advancing means continuing to expand reach for your work. It may seem obvious that you need to sustain effort after a launch campaign for a nonprofit or a new business or product if you want to be successful. But I've noticed that people who launch books do not think about the ongoing effort that comes after the launch.

The advancing phase of any journey to create more reach includes keeping your work alive in online conversations by continuing to create and share value so that people will continue to discover and benefit from your work.

During the advancing phase, the priorities are like those of the building phase: creating new contacts and new connections as you add value through content related to your work. I've displayed the four phases in a circle because I wanted to reinforce the idea that the advancing and building phases are similar and overlap. Both are about creating new opportunities for people to discover and engage with your work.

An Author's Story of Advancing

Charles Bergman and Susan Mann understand the value of investing over the long term in advancing reach for their book or cause. Bergman and Mann, a married couple, created *Every Penguin in the World* as part of a long-term project. Over more than twenty years, they traveled the world to photograph each of the eighteen penguin species in the wild.[1]

KEEPING A BOOK IN THE CONVERSATION
REQUIRES ONGOING CONTENT

To Bergman and Mann, keeping their book in the conversation means "keeping people talking about it, keeping people aware of it, and keeping it visible in some way."[2] Their approach includes two initiatives: Bergman has invested in virtual keynotes and book talks while Mann has focused on creating social media content about their work.

PROMOTING THE CAUSE BEHIND THE BOOK
KEEPS THE MESSAGE FRESH

Mann has discovered that talking about the cause related to the book is a powerful way to connect with their audience. "We are always thinking about keeping the book in the conversation by featuring this cause that we're so passionate about: wild animals, penguins, the natural world," Mann says. "There is this whole environmental message that's very important to us. I'm really thinking about the human being who's looking at Instagram, or LinkedIn, or Facebook, at a post with a penguin photo or a beautiful art Antarctic landscape. When I craft content, I'm thinking about the person receiving the content and what will bring them a moment of joy, what will bring them a piece of information that they can act on. There is something for me there about the human connection that's really important to remember, even when it's all being done virtually and digitally."[3]

GREAT MEDIA COVERAGE HELPS EXTEND REACH

After their book was published, Bergman and Mann continued to devote time, energy, and other resources to expanding the reach of both the book and the larger cause that fuels their passion. Just shy of a year after their book launched, they landed a major media win: a travel feature in the *Washington Post*, both online and on the cover of the Sunday travel section in the print version. This win resulted in a huge spike in sales and lots of interest from their network.

"One of the great surprises of our continuing campaign was that the *Washington Post* did an interview with us, which they published with photos, and that had a huge boost," Bergman said. "That was really terrific. This is the type of media exposure that makes a really big impact. And it sustained it for three weeks. There was a big spike and it hasn't fallen really all the way back at all. And so that's very, very exciting."[4]

When you continue to seek opportunities to share your passion for your book, business, message, cause, or campaign, you can uncover opportunities that you might miss if you cut off your efforts after launch.

**IT'S NATURAL TO SLOW DOWN THE PACE
OF MARKETING AFTER A LAUNCH**

The pace of a launch can be intense and overwhelming and your time, energy, and money resources may evaporate. During this time, it's important to find ways to sustain energy for your overall work. Bergman and Mann plan to continue to focus on this book for quite some time, but they also envision a shift at some point to the next project.

For them, the advancing phase includes creating a sustainable baseline of activities such as ongoing social posting and Amazon advertising that will continue while they explore and create other projects. "We do want to continue to do some things regularly and take the foot off the gas pedal. I mean, maybe go back to 25 miles an hour instead of 100 miles an hour. It's been a pretty intense pace," Mann said.[5]

Quarterly Planning for Activities to Expand the Reach of Any Launch

In addition to continuing to create regular content through what Susan Mann calls "a steady drumbeat on social media" in order to keep your work visible after a launch, there are several ways to keep your work in online conversations, including through ongoing media opportunities, repurposing your content, and showing up consistently with value on social media channels. I recommend looking at your ongoing efforts as a marathon, not a sprint. A launch can feel like a sprint because you go all out for a short period of time. Your ongoing efforts need to be paced appropriately so you can endure over the long haul, and you need to reenergize along the way, much like a marathoner needs fuel and water throughout the race.

Once you're three to six months past the launch, map out key activities to keep growing reach on a quarterly basis. Use the approach Susan Mann mentioned—think beyond the campaign or book you launched to the underlying cause or passion and create content with the people you know will benefit from your work in mind. Here are some possibilities related to a book:

- Specific holiday promotions
- A book-related event, including a discussion group or book club
- A book anniversary celebration
- The release of a new edition of the book; the audio version, for example
- The release of an extra chapter
- The release of a related resource such as a discussion guide
- A Q&A event for readers
- A price promotion on an e-book edition of the book
- A live panel with some of the people featured in the book

Here are some possibilities if you launched a nonprofit cause:

- Create and release a video highlighting the impacts of your fund-raising effort
- Publish articles telling the stories of the impacts of your fund-raising efforts
- Share a photo montage of your work
- Bring together key stakeholders for a virtual or in-person community event

FOR REFLECTION

- Which phase are you in as you contemplate a launch? Are you building, working, launching, or advancing?
- If you are building, what strategies are you using to create deeper relationships with your networks?
- If you are working toward a launch, have you created a timeline of activities between now and launch?
- If you are launching, what celebrations are you planning?
- If you are advancing, what does a sustainable pace look like to you?
- How do you refuel when your energy for your work is lagging?

Additional Resources

Listen to my interview with Charles Bergman and Susan Mann, watch a webinar about the four phases, and download a checklist for marketing a book in each of the four phases.

Notes

INTRODUCTION

1. Jeffrey A. Trachtenberg, "Barack Obama Memoir Sells More Than 887,000 Copies on First Day," *Wall Street Journal*, November 18, 2020, https://www.wsj.com/articles/barack-obama-memoir -sells-more-than-887-000-copies-on-first-day-11605743581.

2. Brené Brown, "Listening to Shame," TED2012 video, March 2012, https://www.ted.com/talks/brene_brown_listening _to_shame.

3. Julie Winkle Guilioni, interview with the author, December 3, 2020.

4. See Grown and Flown Parents Facebook group, https://www .facebook.com/groups/1506637529662997.

5. Tiffany Roe, "Therapy is Cool," https://tiffanyroe.com/

6. Tim Sackett, interview with the author, April 22, 2021.

7. Frank Viola, "Mixing It Up with Ann Voskamp," *Patheos*, February 25, 2013, https://www.patheos.com/blogs/frankviola /annvoskamp/.

8. Jim Neister, "What Steven Burda, 'The Most Connected Person on LinkedIn[,]' Can Teach Us About LinkedIn," *Small Business Trendsetters*, https://smallbusinesstrendsetters.com/what-steven-burda-the-most-connected-person-on-linkedin-can-teach-us-about-linkedin/. For the appellation, see Alexandra Mondelek, "The Most Connected Person on LinkedIn Says He's Going to Take Over the World," *Business Insider*, July 10, 2013, https://www.businessinsider.com/steven-burda-has-most-linkedin-connections-2013-7#:~:text=Steve%20Burda%20Steven%20Burda%20is,direct%20connections%20and%203%2C000%2B%20recommendations.

CHAPTER 1

1. Bronwyn Issac, "Lady Gaga Gets Best Possible Revenge on Ex-Classmates Who Bullied Her with a Facebook Group," *Upworthy*, May 8, 2019, https://www.upworthy.com/lady-gaga-gets-best-possible-revenge-on-ex-classmates-who-bullied-her-with-a-facebook-group.

2. Neil McCormick, "Lady Gaga: 'I've always been famous, you just didn't know it,'" *The Telegraph*, February 16, 2010, https://www.telegraph.co.uk/culture/music/rockandpopfeatures/7221051/Lady-Gaga-Ive-always-been-famous-you-just-didnt-know-it.html.

3. The quotes in this section are from Beverly Kaye, interview with the author, April 22, 2021.

4. The quotes in this section are from Karin Hurt, interview with the author, April 20, 2021.

CHAPTER 2

1. The quotes in this section are from Lisa Kohn, interview with the author, March 17, 2021.

2. Cheryl Rice, interview with author, February 22, 2021.

3. Dan Rockwell, interview with the author, December 16, 2020.

CHAPTER 3

1. The quotes in this section are from Mark Miller, interview with the author, April 16, 2021.

CHAPTER 4

1. David Cooperrider, interview with the author, June 24, 2021.

2. David Cooperrider, interview with the author.

3. David Cooperrider, interview with the author.

4. David Cooperrider, interview with the author.

5. David Cooperrider, interview with the author.

6. David Cooperrider, interview with the author.

7. Ron Fry, interview with the author, June 28, 2021.

8. Wendy Ryan, interview with the author, July 30, 2021.

9. Fauzia Burke, interview with the author, August 19, 2021.

10. "Definition & Facts for Celiac Disease," National Institute of Diabetes and Digestive and Kidney Diseases, https://www .niddk.nih.gov/health-information/digestive-diseases/celiac -disease/definition-facts.

11. Ron Fry, interview with the author.

12. David Cooperrider, interview with the author.

13. Karin Hurt, interview with the author, April 20, 2021.

14. Chris Brogan, interview with the author, May 12, 2021.

15. Chris Brogan, interview with the author.

16. Chris Brogan, interview with the author.

17. David Cooperrider, interview with the author.

18. Karin Hurt, interview with the author.

19. David Cooperrider, interview with the author.

CHAPTER 5

1. Chris Brogan, interview with the author, May 12, 2021.

2. Sabrina Horn, interview with the author, April 22, 2021.

3. Chris Brogan, interview with the author.

CHAPTER 6

1. Jon Gordon, interview with the author, April 19, 2021.

2. Daniel Decker, "Jon Gordan," May 15, 2015, in author's possession.

3. Jon Gordon, interview with the author.

4. Jon Gordon, interview with the author.

5. Jon Gordon, interview with the author.

6. Whitney Johnson, interview with the author, December 10, 2020.

7. Chris Brogan, "How to Engineer an Outcome in Emails," January 24, 2021, in author's possession.

CHAPTER 7

1. Jim McQueen, email to the author, October 15, 2021.

2. Jennifer Bangs, interview with the author, April 6, 2021.

CHAPTER 8

1. Lisa Fain, interview with the author, February 9, 2021.

2. Husna Haq, "What Oprah Has Done for Books," *Christian Science Monitor*, May 24, 2011, https://www.csmonitor.com/Books /chapter-and-verse/2011/0524/What-Oprah-has-done-for -books.

3. Sandy Smith, "The Big Leagues," July 6, 2021, in author's possession.

CHAPTER 9

1. Joseph Epstein, "Think You Have a Book in You? Think Again," *New York Times*, September 28, 2002, https://www.nytimes .com/2002/09/28/opinion/think-you-have-a-book-in-you -think-again.html.

2. Tim Sackett, interview with the author, April 22, 2021.

3. Mark Miller, interview with the author, April 16, 2021.

4. Tessa Trudeau, "Olympic Long-Distance Runner Alexi Pappas Talks Training, Team Spirit and How She Came to Love Her Sport—and Inspires Us to Lace Up Our Own Running Shoes," *Nordstrom,* https://www.nordstrom.com/browse/style-guide /fashion-news/lifestyle/alexi-pappas-interview.

5. Rachel Thompson, "A Woman Is Writing Poignant Poems to Strangers Based on Their Twitter DMs," *Mashable*, November 29, 2017, https://mashable.com/article/morgan-harper -nichols-poetry.

6. Justin Miller, interview with the author, June 29, 2021.

7. "About Us," charity:water, https://www.charitywater.org/about.

8. Steven Piersanti, "The 10 Awful Truths about Book Publishing," *Berrett-Koehler Publishers,* June 24, 2020, https://ideas .bkconnection.com/10-awful-truths-about-publishing.

9. Mark Miller, interview with the author.

10. Todd Sattersten, interview with the author, May 5, 2021.

11. Todd Sattersten, interview with the author.

12. Todd Sattersten, interview with the author.

CHAPTER 10

1. Emma Wenner, "Jennifer Lopez's Daughter Debuts with Book on Prayer," *Publisher's Weekly*, May 20, 2020, https://www .publishersweekly.com/pw/by-topic/industry-news/religion /article/83366-jennifer-lopez-s-daughter-debuts-with-book -on-prayer.html.

2. Richard Jean So and Gus Wezerek, "Just How White Is the Book Industry?," *New York Times*, December 11, 2020, https://www .nytimes.com/interactive/2020/12/11/opinion/culture/diversity -publishing-industry.html.

3. Minal Bopaiah, interview with the author, June 28, 2021.

4. Jenn T. Grace, interview with the author, April 30, 2021.

5. Barbara Roose, interview with the author, June 9, 2021.

6. Justin Miller, interview with the author, June 29, 2021.

7. Justin Miller, interview with the author.

8. Justin Miller, interview with the author.

9. Minal Bopaiah, interview with the author.

10. Ann Byle, "Agents of Color See Changes, Challenges in Christian Publishing," *Publishers Weekly*, April 21, 2021, https://www.publishersweekly.com/pw/by-topic/industry-news/religion/article/86117-agents-of-color-see-changes-challenges-in-christian-publishing.html.

11. Minal Bopaiah, interview with the author.

12. Minal Bopaiah, interview with the author.

13. Natalie Nixon, 2021 Berrett-Kohler Nonfiction Book Marketing Workshop, April 30, 2021.

14. Arthur Woods, interview with the author, September 7, 2021.

CONCLUSION

1. Justin Miller, interview with the author, June 29, 2021.

2. Justin Miller, interview with the author.

3. Ronne Rock, Instagram post, June 30, 2021.

APPENDIX

1. Charles Bergman and Susan Mann, interview with the author, April 5, 2021.

2. Charles Bergman and Susan Mann, interview with the author.

3. Charles Bergman and Susan Mann, interview with the author.

4. Charles Bergman and Susan Mann, interview with the author.

5. Charles Bergman and Susan Mann, interview with the author.

Acknowledgments

What an author most wants is for people to read, apply, and take action as a result of their work. If you have read my book and plan to apply it, thank you!

I'm blessed to have had so many people who have championed my journey to publication.

I'm very grateful to my family: my husband, Eric, and Cam, Natalie, and Maggie. A love of writing connected Eric and me in the beginning and I'm glad, thirty years after he read my college writing, that he's still willing to read my work and help me make it better. Cam has been proofreading and giving feedback on my work since third grade.

My mother and Henry ignited and fueled my love of books and writing over the years. I appreciate their unconditional kindness to me, including how they cheered me on as I completed this book. Thanks to my successful and ambitious older brothers, Byron Bassett and Lieutenant General David Bassett, for always being there for me. I'm so proud of both of you.

Twelve years ago, we moved from Chicago to the Toledo, Ohio, area to be closer to my in-laws and extended family. I'm so glad we did. Thank you for weekly Sunday lunches and to my father-in-law for asking about my progress with the book all along the way.

Jesse Lyn Stoner introduced me to my first client at Weaving Influence (Whitney Johnson), one of my first team members (Margy Kerr-Jarrett), and Berrett-Koehler Publishers/BK Authors. All three of these introductions have had a substantial impact on my life. This book would not exist in quite the same way—if at all—if those introductions had not happened. Whitney, thank you for your confidence in me and for your support, both personal and professional, over the years.

The members of the team at Berrett-Koehler Publishers are true partners and dear friends. I am so glad I had the chance to work with them on my book after collaborating on so many projects over the past decade. Kristen Frantz, Katie Sheehan, and Michael Crowley championed my book proposal; Neal Maillet patiently listened to pitch after pitch and gave me a yes at the right time. I've been honored to support Johanna Vondeling and David Marshall and to have their support for my work. Big thanks as well to Jeevan Sivasubramaniam, Zoe Mackey, Leslie Crandell, Charlotte Ashlock, Lesley Iura, Valerie Caldwell, and Steve Piersanti.

I met Kate Babbitt, my copy editor, later in the journey. She describes the job of a copy editor as being a "wingwoman" and I've truly experienced her support in that way. A good editor is a true gift. Thank you, Kate.

I'm grateful every day for the team at Weaving Influence. Amy Driehorst and Christy Kirk share leadership with me and give me space to create and dream.

Carrie Koens, one of the first contractors I hired, has been encouraging me to write a book for years, never letting me lose sight of my own goals and dreams. She read and gave editorial suggestions throughout this process, always pushing me to share *my* perspectives. Kelly Griffin handled many of the behind-the-scenes project management details that would have otherwise left me confounded, including endnotes and formatting. Thank you, Kelly, for always being willing to say yes to coffee and queso (not together, though!).

When your team launches books for a living, it's important to plan and execute your own book launch flawlessly. Aubrey Pastorek, I'm so grateful for your focused and diligent work on my book launch.

The entire Weaving Influence team is a gift. I appreciate Lindsey Vandervlucht's management of my social media channels; Kristin Elliot's work to oversee my social media strategy; Isabel Thornton, who supports our podcast; Lise Stevens/Elizabeth Mars, our talented PR professionals, who have expanded media opportunities for me and my book; Kelly Edmiston, who manages projects with excellence and coordinates Team Buzz Builder; Wendy Haan, a constant encourager and project manager; Lori Weidert, who brings a wealth of book production expertise; Sarah Kocinski, who keeps so many operations tasks running smoothly; and Amanda Hugo, who has done and will do nearly any support task imaginable to ensure that our team is well served. Deirdre Honner joined our team during the writing of this book, bringing invaluable HR expertise, careful listening, and unparalleled kindness and support.

Over the years, Rachel Royer has made all our clients' work better through her artful and beautiful design work.

I'm so grateful for her beautiful work designing my book cover, interior graphics, and website. Karin Tome, thank you for hanging in there during some challenging times of managing websites at Weaving Influence and for your amazing work and friendship. Russ Hawkins, thank you for your work to bring the new beckyrobinson.com to life.

We have the privilege of collaborating with others who also work in the book and marketing business. Thank you to Fauzia Burke, Sandy Smith, Todd Sattersten, Rajat Kapur/ Tina DePrisco, Sharon Goldinger, Tina Dietz, Jenn T. Grace, Cathy Fyock, and Rusty Shelton, who have all generously shared encouragement, wisdom, and best practices.

To Trena White of Page Two Books: I love working with you and the way our teams' values align so well. Thank you for continuing to discover ways to partner with my team.

I'm grateful for the clients who choose to partner with the Weaving Influence team, including long-term clients Chip Bell, Susan Fowler, Lisa Fain, Bob Tiede, Beau Sides, Bonnie Marcus, Julie Winkle Giulioni, Mark Miller, and the team at Next Element.

In addition to these long-term clients, many people I've met on my journey have coached and encouraged me and my team in formal and informal ways, including Susan Mazza, Mary Jo Asmus, Mike Henry Sr., Phil Gerbyshak, David Taylor-Klaus, Eileen McDargh, Jane Anderson, Nate Regier, Joan McArthur-Blair, Bev Kaye, and Jennifer Kahnweiler.

To all the people mentioned in and interviewed for this book—I'm honored by the time and attention you gave. I learn from you daily.

Every week, thousands of people open and read my Friday email. If you are among my readers, thank you! I also thank the hundreds of people who participate in book launches as part of Team Buzz Builder by supporting our clients with Amazon reviews and social media posts.

The Running Buds have been an amazing support. Thanks to Colleen Warner, one of the group's founders, for keeping us all going during the pandemic and to Kary Whearty, Lauri Cooper, Holly Stuard, Alexis Smith, Marina Ederra, Sharon Pilaski, and Kathleen Drummonds for encouragement in writing, running, and life.

My friend Sarah Nocella welcomed me into her life, sharing the joy of her daughter/my bonus daughter Macy. Through Sarah, we met the Michigan grandparents for our kids, Tom and Ginny Nocella, who bless us with love, prayers, and breakfast cookies. Thank you!

Special thanks to Sarah Douglas and Lisa Weber for their enduring friendship and support.

Other prayer warriors and encouragers who have supported me include Judy Douglass, Danise DiStasi, Tammy Doci, Kourtney Street, Barb Roose, Laura Finch, and Gary/ Carol Knosp.

My friend Jamie Mahurin Smith is a daily support and encouragement who is often the first and last person to text me every day. She is a true gift and I'm so grateful we reconnected after so many years.

Index

Note: Figures are indicated by *f*.

About the Author

Becky Robinson is the founder and CEO of Weaving Influence (weavinginfluence.com), a full-service digital marketing agency that specializes in supporting authors, business leaders, coaches, trainers, speakers, and thought leaders. Weaving Influence, which was founded in 2012, offers services that include strategic con-sultation/coaching for authors and thought leaders, social media management, public relations, virtual meeting facilitation, and book launch services. Under Becky's leadership, the firm has worked with clients on more than 150 book launches that have enabled authors to build their brands, acquire more business customers, and increase book sales.

Becky hosts *The Book Marketing Action Podcast*, where she shares actionable advice to help authors achieve their goals of reaching more readers and enhancing their brands. She has created many resources and events to help authors, including the Reach More Readers Workshop.

Becky has an MA in intercultural studies from Wheaton College and a BA in English and creative writing from Miami University. When she's not working or writing, Becky is a distance runner. She has completed ten full and eleven half marathons. She also ran 50K to celebrate her fiftieth birthday. Becky and her husband of nearly thirty years live in Lambertville, Michigan. They have three children.

Berrett–Koehler
Publishers

Berrett-Koehler is an independent publisher dedicated to an ambitious mission: *Connecting people and ideas to create a world that works for all.*

Our publications span many formats, including print, digital, audio, and video. We also offer online resources, training, and gatherings. And we will continue expanding our products and services to advance our mission.

We believe that the solutions to the world's problems will come from all of us, working at all levels: in our society, in our organizations, and in our own lives. Our publications and resources offer pathways to creating a more just, equitable, and sustainable society. They help people make their organizations more humane, democratic, diverse, and effective (and we don't think there's any contradiction there). And they guide people in creating positive change in their own lives and aligning their personal practices with their aspirations for a better world.

And we strive to practice what we preach through what we call "The BK Way." At the core of this approach is *stewardship,* a deep sense of responsibility to administer the company for the benefit of all of our stakeholder groups, including authors, customers, employees, investors, service providers, sales partners, and the communities and environment around us. Everything we do is built around stewardship and our other core values of *quality, partnership, inclusion,* and *sustainability.*

This is why Berrett-Koehler is the first book publishing company to be both a B Corporation (a rigorous certification) and a benefit corporation (a for-profit legal status), which together require us to adhere to the highest standards for corporate, social, and environmental performance. And it is why we have instituted many pioneering practices (which you can learn about at www.bkconnection.com), including the Berrett-Koehler Constitution, the Bill of Rights and Responsibilities for BK Authors, and our unique Author Days.

We are grateful to our readers, authors, and other friends who are supporting our mission. We ask you to share with us examples of how BK publications and resources are making a difference in your lives, organizations, and communities at www.bkconnection.com/impact.

Dear reader,

Thank you for picking up this book and welcome to the worldwide BK community! You're joining a special group of people who have come together to create positive change in their lives, organizations, and communities.

What's BK all about?

Our mission is to connect people and ideas to create a world that works for all.

Why? Our communities, organizations, and lives get bogged down by old paradigms of self-interest, exclusion, hierarchy, and privilege. But we believe that can change. That's why we seek the leading experts on these challenges—and share their actionable ideas with you.

A welcome gift

To help you get started, we'd like to offer you a **free copy** of one of our bestselling ebooks:

www.bkconnection.com/welcome

When you claim your **free ebook**, you'll also be subscribed to our blog.

Our freshest insights

Access the best new tools and ideas for leaders at all levels on our blog at ideas.bkconnection.com.

Sincerely,

Your friends at Berrett-Koehler